IMAGES
of Rail

THE TOLEDO, PEORIA & WESTERN RAILWAY

This map shows the entire Toledo, Peoria & Western (TP&W) Railway system. As of 2022, another company, the Keokuk Junction Railway, now owns the railroad west of Peoria but the railroad east of Peoria is still owned and operated by the TP&W. East of Logansport, Indiana, the TP&W currently leases the Winamac & Southern Railway to gain access to the city of Kokomo. (Map by the author.)

On the Cover: Taken in the early 1940s, this photograph shows a freight train crew posing in front of a caboose. From left to right are Leon Page, two unidentified, Herman Brenken, and Leo Clark. (Courtesy of the Clark/Finson Collection, Special Collections Center, Bradley University Library.)

IMAGES
of Rail

THE TOLEDO,
PEORIA & WESTERN
RAILWAY

Thomas Dyrek

ARCADIA
PUBLISHING

Published by Arcadia Publishing
Charleston, South Carolina

Library of Congress Control Number: 2022931424

For all general information, please contact Arcadia Publishing:
Telephone 843-853-2070
Fax 843-853-0044
E-mail sales@arcadiapublishing.com
For customer service and orders:
Toll-Free 1-888-313-2665

Visit us on the Internet at www.arcadiapublishing.com

*In memory of Roger Holmes,
TP&W dispatcher, photographer, and historian.*

CONTENTS

ACKNOWLEDGMENTS

Anyone who has a serious interest in railroading or railroad history has a favorite railroad company. For me, that railroad is the Toledo, Peoria & Western. I had been aware of the TP&W for most of my life as it was (and still is) one of the railroads that passes through my local area. As I started to become interested in the history of railroading, my grandmother told me that we had TP&W in our blood—my third great-grandfather was a brakeman and conductor for them during the 1870s. By the time I was in high school, I had some TP&W models on my train set and a rapidly growing collection of slides and negatives of TP&W trains. During my sophomore year, I was informed that there was a historical society dedicated to the TP&W. I inquired about joining the organization, but much to my disappointment, I was told that it went defunct several years before when its president had passed away. A couple of weeks later, I decided to see if there would be any interest in a new society. The response was overwhelming. I cranked out the first newsletter in December 2018 and since then, the TP&W Historical Society has grown considerably. We now have dozens of members from all over the world, including several former TP&W employees. Through our members, historical documents, extensive research, and interviews conducted with TP&W employees and fans, I have gathered lots of fascinating information, pictures, and stories that I look forward to sharing with you in this book. I would like to thank the following people and organizations for their assistance: John Stell, Roger Holmes, David Jordan, Harold Krewer, Dean Cunningham, Larry Miller Jr., Jason Jordan, Rick Burn, Dave Arganbright, Thomas Waldon, Matt Smith, Connor Taylor, John and Roger Kujawa, Jesse Berryhill, Steve Smedley, Brandon Osika, Noah Haggerty, the Keokuk Public Library, the Cullom-Davis Library at Bradley University, my friends and family, and the staff at Arcadia Publishing.

INTRODUCTION

Ask just about anyone familiar with the Toledo, Peoria & Western about the railroad, and chances are the response will include one of the TP&W's many nicknames that it received over the years: "Tired, Proven & Willing," "Two Ponies & Wagon," "Tippy-Wobbly," "Tip-Up," "Tired, Poor & Weary," and others. These names all originated over the many years of the TP&W's existence and have been passed around among railroad employees, railfans, and the general public alike.

The earliest known nickname of the TP&W was "Tired, Poor & Weary," which appears to have originated in the late 1880s after a tragic train wreck at Chatsworth, Illinois, on August 10, 1887, from which subsequent lawsuits almost shut the railroad down. The 1887 wreck was not the beginning of the TP&W's struggles, however. Then 38 years old, the railroad had been plagued with issues from very early on, which resulted in several mergers, sales, and reorganizations throughout the 19th century.

It all started on February 12, 1849, when the Peoria & Oquawka (P&O) Railroad Company was chartered. At the time, railroads were still very new to the state of Illinois, and the P&O was one of the first in the area. Construction began in 1851. The railroad was intended to connect Peoria, Illinois, with the Mississippi River at Oquawka, Illinois, but, for reasons unknown, the village of Oquawka was not interested in having a railroad in their town and forced the P&O to find another western terminus. The P&O then began to build its line to nearby Burlington, Iowa, instead.

In 1852, the P&O began building east from Peoria as well, with the goal of reaching the Illinois/Indiana state line at Effner, Indiana. During this time, the P&O was loaned some money by the Central Military Tract Railroad (CMTRR) to complete a section of track between Peoria and Burlington. The P&O was unable to pay back the loan, and as a result, the CMTRR's predecessor, the Chicago, Burlington & Quincy Railroad, took over the P&O's Peoria-to-Burlington route as compensation.

The Peoria-to-Effner route remained under the P&O's ownership, and train service on that line finally began on January 11, 1860. However, by this time, the P&O was in extreme debt and fell into financial trouble. The railroad was sold to the Logansport, Peoria & Burlington Railroad (LP&B) in late 1860. This new owner was very short-lived; it too fell into financial problems after just a couple of years of operation. Soon after, the line went through another reorganization.

On October 16, 1864, the Toledo, Peoria & Warsaw Railway Company was formed to take over the railroad. This new company did well financially for several years and was able to successfully construct a new western route linking Peoria with the Mississippi River at Keokuk, Iowa. A branch line was built from Hamilton to Warsaw, Illinois. However, the Toledo, Peoria & Warsaw also eventually entered bankruptcy. On December 16, 1879, another new company, the Toledo, Peoria & Western Railroad, took over the property. Soon after, the TP&W was leased to the Wabash Railroad, which entered bankruptcy in 1884.

In early 1887, the TP&W was sold at foreclosure to a new company that kept the TP&W name but switched from "Toledo, Peoria & Western Railroad" to "Toledo, Peoria & Western Railway." This new company managed to stay afloat through the remainder of the 19th century, despite several major challenges like the Chatsworth wreck of 1887 mentioned earlier. These years of hard times resulted in the "Tired, Poor & Weary" nickname.

"Tippy-Wobbly," a more modern nickname, came to be in the early 1920s. A few years before, the TP&W had started struggling again and entered bankruptcy in 1917. It was taken over by the US government in an effort to keep the railroad open to help with the war effort during World War I. However, under the government's control, the railroad's financial and physical condition rapidly worsened, and when it was returned to private ownership in 1920, it was on its last legs. Trains, tracks, and structures were in very poor condition, and the railroad was almost to the point of ceasing operations. Trains "tipped" and "wobbled" on deteriorating track, which earned the railroad its new nickname.

In 1926, the railroad was sold to George McNear, a businessman from New York who quickly went to work improving it. McNear was successful in this effort, and thanks to him, the railroad survived the Great Depression. However, while McNear was successful at rebuilding the railroad, he was just the opposite when it came to having a positive relationship with his employees. During the 1920s, 1930s, and 1940s, the TP&W was plagued with dozens of bitter strikes and other related problems. This came to an abrupt end when McNear was killed in 1947 during a violent strike on the railroad. Shortly after his death, new management was appointed, and peace was made. The new management continued to help the company prosper, and the TP&W did very well through the 1950s and 1960s. Around 1960, a newer and more positive nickname, "Tip-Up," emerged.

Sadly, these good times were not to last. The TP&W once again fell on hard times during the 1970s, and in 1981, it became a subsidiary of the Santa Fe Railway. At the end of 1983, the Santa Fe absorbed the TP&W completely, ending a 135-year history. The Santa Fe operated the former TP&W tracks until 1989, when it was sold to a new company that revived the TP&W name. The "reincarnated" TP&W was sold to a holding company in 1996, and over the following decade and a half was sold two more times. At the time of this writing in 2021, the TP&W is owned by Genesee & Wyoming, a holding company that owns and operates multiple railroads around the world. While it may not be the same as it was decades ago, the TP&W remains an important part of local railroading, serving many businesses and industries.

The Toledo, Peoria & Western Railway covers the history of the Tired, Poor & Weary, Tippy-Wobbly, Tip-Up, or whatever one wishes to call it, from the beginning of the Peoria & Oquawka in 1849 to the present day. Many historical photographs, some of which have never been made available to the public before, stories from former railroad employees, and lots of fascinating information help make this book a great one for any railroad or history fan. It is hoped that you will enjoy it and learn some interesting things about this very unique railroad.

One

THE EARLY YEARS

On February 12, 1849, a group of businessmen from western Illinois chartered the Peoria & Oquawka Railroad Company to construct a railroad west from Peoria on the Illinois River to Oquawka on the Mississippi River. However, the village of Oquawka was not interested in having a railroad, so the P&O built its tracks to nearby Burlington, Iowa, instead. An eastern route from Peoria to Effner was also constructed, and train service on that line began on January 11, 1860. During this construction phase, the P&O was loaned money by the Central Military Tract Railroad to complete a portion of the Peoria-to-Burlington route. The P&O used most of its finances to complete the construction and was unable to pay back the CMTRR's loan. As a result, its Peoria-to-Burlington line was seized. The subsequent financial issues from this began a series of mergers, sales, and reorganizations of the railroad and the companies that owned it. In late 1860, the railroad was sold to the Logansport, Peoria & Burlington, and in 1864, it became the Toledo, Peoria & Warsaw. The Toledo, Peoria & Warsaw did well early on and was able to construct a new western route out of Peoria to Keokuk to replace the one from Peoria to Burlington. However, this company also fell on hard times in the 1870s and could not continue. In 1879, it became the Toledo, Peoria & Western Railroad, and in 1887, it was reorganized one more time as the Toledo, Peoria & Western Railway. Despite some challenges, this final company was able to stay afloat and survived into the 20th century.

This 1856 bond for the Peoria & Oquawka is one of the few surviving pieces of P&O paperwork. Ever since the P&O ceased to exist as a company in 1861, many of the documents and paperwork were lost to fires or floods, or simply thrown away. Today, Peoria & Oquawka items are extremely rare and highly sought after by railroad and history buffs. (Author's collection.)

LOGANSPORT, PEORIA & BURLINGTON

RAILWAY.

1860.  1860.

Formerly Peoria & Oquawka (Eastern Extension) R. R.

BETWEEN

PEORIA, ILL., AND LOGANSPORT, IND., 171 1-2 MILES.

This Road is now completed and running regularly between the above points, forming, with its connections, the shortest Line, either constructed or projected, between the Mississippi River and the Atlantic Seaboard.

CONNECTIONS ARE AS FOLLOWS:

At PEORIA, with the Peoria, Oquawka & Burlington R. R.
At EL PASO, with the Illinois Central (Main Line) Railroad.
At CHENOA, with the St. Louis, Alton & Chicago Railroad.
At GILMAN, with the Illinois Central (Branch) Railroad.
At REYNOLDS, with Louisville, N. Albany & Chicago R. R.
At LOGANSPORT, { with the Toledo & Wabash Railroad,
              { with the Chicago & Cincinnati R. R.

EXPRESS PASSENGER AND FREIGHT TRAINS

Will be run over this Line of Road, with no change of cars between Burlington, Iowa, and Toledo and Cincinnati. Its short distance, in comparison with competing Lines, ensures regular connections, allowing quick time without excessive or dangerous speed.

Rates for Passengers & Freight always as low as by any other Route

SLEEPING CARS ON ALL NIGHT TRAINS.

Merchants and Forwarders will note the advantage of having their goods transported between Toledo or Cincinnati and Burlington, without changing cars or breaking bulk.

Apply to all regular Agents at Boston, New York, Philadelphia, Baltimore, Cincinnati, Chicago, or other prominent points, for rates or further information.

WM. H. CRUGER, Sup't.

CHAS. E. FOLLETT, Gen'l Freight and Ticket Agent, Peoria.
WM. H. BACKUS, Gen'l Western Agent, Burlington, Iowa.
T. A. H. SMYTHE, Gen'l Agent, Logansport.
GEO. R. WEED, Gen'l Eastern Agent, Rutland, Vt.

12

This advertisement is from the Logansport, Peoria & Burlington Railroad. The LP&B owned track from Logansport to Effner, where a connection with the Peoria & Oquawka was located. When the P&O shut down in 1860, the LP&B acquired the former P&O tracks from Effner to Peoria. The LP&B began to suffer financial problems very early on and only operated until 1864, when the Toledo, Peoria & Warsaw took over the property. Eventually, the Pennsylvania Railroad acquired the tracks east of Effner, while the Toledo, Peoria & Warsaw retained ownership west of Effner. (Author's collection.)

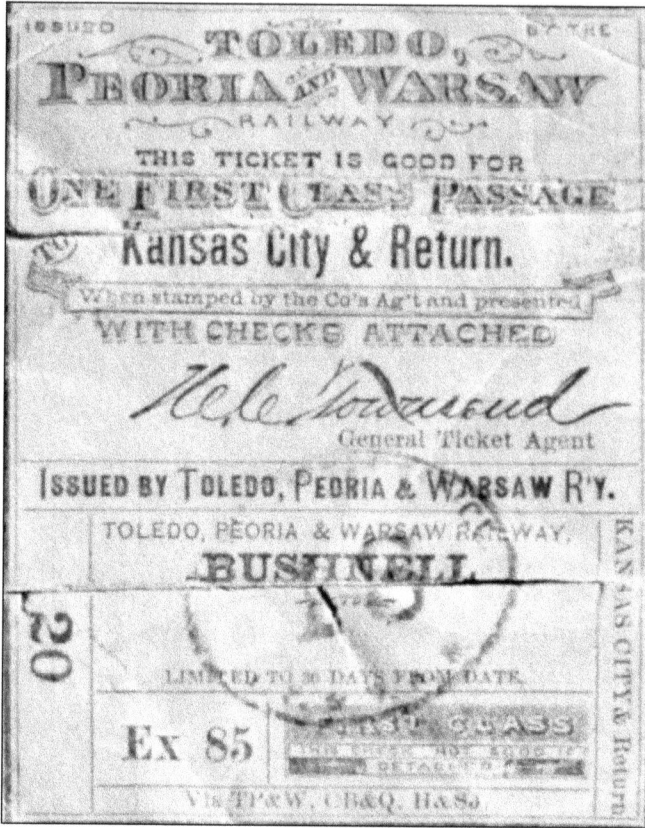

Passenger train tickets, such as this one from Bushnell, Illinois, could be purchased at any depot along the Toledo, Peoria & Western and its predecessors. This particular ticket from the Toledo, Peoria & Warsaw era allowed its owner to change trains at the western end of the railroad and travel on a different railroad to Kansas City without having to buy another ticket. (Author's collection.)

This photograph shows a Toledo, Peoria & Warsaw steam locomotive at an early depot in Peoria, which was likely built during the Peoria & Oquawka era of the 1850s. The date of this photograph is unknown, though it is suspected to be from the early 1870s. (Courtesy of the Paul H. Stringham Collection, Special Collections Center, Bradley University Library.)

Charles Orlando Scovill was a brakeman and later a conductor on the Toledo, Peoria & Warsaw during the 1870s. He lived in Peoria within walking distance of the railroad's yard on Persimmon Street. A veteran of the Civil War, Scovill later relocated to Leavenworth, Kansas, to work on other railroads. He passed away on June 1, 1923. (Courtesy of Susie Pope.)

Throughout its history, the Toledo, Peoria & Western and its predecessor companies owned several unique locomotives. This experimental engine of the mid-1800s was built with two smokestacks instead of one in an attempt to improve efficiency. The experiment was unsuccessful, and the engine was later rebuilt with a traditional single stack. (Courtesy of the Paul H. Stringham Collection, Special Collections Center, Bradley University Library.)

13

On the night of August 10, 1887, the recently reorganized Toledo, Peoria & Western experienced a tragic train wreck. Earlier in the day, a wooden trestle bridge just east of Chatsworth, Illinois, caught fire. The bridge did not collapse, but it was greatly weakened. A few hours after the fire, which had not been seen by anyone, a special eastbound excursion train carrying about 500 vacationers from Peoria to Niagara Falls, New York, began to cross the bridge. The first of two locomotives pulling the train made it over, but the bridge collapsed under the weight of the rest of the train. At the time, most passenger cars were made of wood. Because of this, the destruction of the cars as the train derailed was extreme. In addition to multiple fires breaking out, several cars "telescoped," meaning that the force of the wreck shoved cars on top of one another. The Chatsworth wreck claimed the lives of over 80 people and injured hundreds more. The many lawsuits filed following the wreck almost drove the railroad into bankruptcy. (Courtesy of Larry Miller Jr.)

In the wake of the Chatsworth wreck, railroads began adopting safer technology. Bridges made of steel, stone, and concrete were built, and wooden passenger cars were phased out in favor of stronger and safer cars made of steel. In 1954, the State of Illinois placed a historical marker commemorating the wreck along US Route 24 just south of the wreck site. (Photograph by the author.)

THE CHATSWORTH WRECK
MIDNIGHT, AUGUST 10-11,1887
ONE HALF MILE NORTH ON THE
TOLEDO, PEORIA & WESTERN
RAILROAD OCCURRED ONE OF THE
WORST WRECKS IN AMERICAN RAIL
HISTORY. AN EXCURSION TRAIN-TWO
ENGINES AND APPROXIMATELY
TWENTY WOODEN COACHES - FROM
PEORIA TO NIAGARA FALLS.
STRUCK A BURNING CULVERT. OF THE
500 PASSENGERS ABOUT 85
PERISHED AND SCORES WERE
INJURED.
ERECTED BY THE STATE OF ILLINOIS
1954.

This photograph from the late 1800s shows an early 4-4-0 type steam locomotive in Peoria. "4-4-0" is the locomotive's wheel arrangement, meaning it has four small wheels up front to support the front of the locomotive, four large "driver" wheels in the middle to power the locomotive, and no additional wheels behind the drivers. (Courtesy of the Paul H. Stringham Collection, Special Collections Center, Bradley University Library.)

This photograph from the 1890s shows an eastbound passenger train making a stop at Glasford, Illinois, west of Peoria. The Glasford depot was built in the 1880s and remained in service until 1956, after which it was torn down. Fred Harding served as the Glasford station agent for many years. (Author's collection.)

By the end of the 19th century, locomotive technology had advanced considerably, and newer, larger locomotives were being built and placed into service. Locomotive No. 5 was a 2-8-0 type engine (two small wheels up front, eight big driver wheels in the middle, and no additional wheels in the back). (Courtesy of the Paul H. Stringham Collection, Special Collections Center, Bradley University Library.)

Two

A New Century

By 1900, the Toledo, Peoria & Western was doing very well. New locomotives and cars were purchased, new stations and other company buildings were constructed, and the railroad's finances were in a good state. Experienced railroaders such as Edwin Armstrong, Edward F. Leonard, and Samuel Russel served as presidents of the railroad during this time, and helped the company prosper for several years. However, this came to an end in 1917 when the TP&W once again fell on hard times and entered receivership. On December 28, 1917, the railroad was taken over by the United States Railroad Administration (USRA), a government-owned and operated organization that took over many railroad companies in the United States during the wartime period of the late 1910s in an effort to improve the efficiency of railroad service. The TP&W was returned to private ownership in February 1920, but unfortunately, it had become a victim of the USRA's inability to properly operate certain railroads during the war. The company was left in very poor financial condition, and the property itself was in bad shape, with deteriorating track, equipment, and buildings. Almost to the point of being unable to continue operations, many wondered if it was going to be able to survive. The TP&W was once again "Tired, Poor & Weary."

In 1905, the Toledo, Peoria & Western acquired ten 4-6-0 type locomotives from the Baldwin Locomotive Works of Philadelphia, Pennsylvania. This photograph shows the fifth engine of the group, No. 54, shortly after it was built. (Courtesy of the Paul H. Stringham Collection, Special Collections Center, Bradley University Library.)

This photograph, taken on July 19, 1910, shows a wreck on the TP&W at Bartonville, Illinois, just south of Peoria. Some coal cars that were parked at a nearby hospital power plant started rolling uncontrollably out of the plant and onto the main line. A short time later, they were struck by a passenger train. (Courtesy of Dean Cunningham.)

18

The western terminus for many passenger trains on the TP&W was Keokuk Union Depot in Keokuk, Iowa, just west of the Mississippi River. Keokuk Union Depot was built in 1891 and also served trains on the Rock Island, Wabash, and Chicago, Burlington & Quincy Railroads. It was designed by famous Chicago architect John Wellborn Root. After the last passenger train left the station in 1967, it was used by the four railroads previously mentioned as an office building for their agents. Over the years, Keokuk Union Depot saw various other railroad uses before being loaned to the City of Keokuk in 2011. It was listed in the National Register of Historic Places on March 27, 2013. As of 2021, the building is being renovated for use as a museum, community center, and event venue. (Author's collection.)

The Fairbury Union Depot was built in 1904 to replace an earlier structure that dated to the mid-1800s. In addition to TP&W trains, the depot also served trains from the Wabash Railroad. It was demolished in 1934. Salvaged bricks from the site were used to construct a church nearby. (Author's collection.)

Gilman, Illinois, is situated at a junction between the TP&W and Illinois Central Railroad. In 1909, this depot was constructed at the junction to serve passenger trains on both railroads. Passenger trains do not stop here anymore, but the building remains in use as an office and storage facility for the railroad. (Photograph by the author.)

This photograph from 1915 shows the TP&W roundhouse at Effner, Indiana. Roundhouses were special facilities designed to house and maintain steam locomotives. The roundhouse in this photograph was built around 1880 to replace an earlier structure that had badly deteriorated. As the TP&W progressed into the 20th century, it was determined that this facility was no longer needed, and it was demolished prior to 1940. (Author's collection.)

In 1904, the TP&W and the New York Central Railroad built this station in Sheldon, Illinois, at a junction where the two lines crossed each other. Two years later, an identical station was built in nearby Watseka at another junction between the TP&W and the Chicago & Eastern Illinois Railroad. (Author's collection.)

This early-1900s photograph shows the Toledo, Peoria & Western's depot at Cuba, Illinois, west of Peoria. Nearby, the TP&W crossed the Fulton County Narrow Gauge (FCNG), a local railroad that ran from West Havana to Galesburg, Illinois. Unlike most railroads whose rails are four feet, eight and one-half inches apart, the FCNG's rails were only three feet apart. (Courtesy of John Stell.)

The depot at Chenoa, Illinois, located at a junction between the TP&W and Chicago & Alton Railroads, was built in the winter of 1918 to replace an earlier structure that was destroyed by fire. The fire is believed to have been started by fireworks during celebrations for the end of World War I. (Author's collection.)

Three

THE MCNEAR ERA

By 1925, the Toledo, Peoria & Western was on its last legs both physically and financially. In 1926, the State of Illinois ordered the sale of the struggling railroad. After failing to attract any buyers, it was finally sold at auction to New York businessman George P. McNear Jr. on July 11, 1926, for $1.3 million. The deal was finalized in 1927, and soon after, McNear went to work bringing the railroad back up to high standards. Throughout the 1920s and 1930s, many improvements and changes were made. However, not all was well. McNear had become notorious for refusing to raise wages or improve working conditions for his employees. Strikes began in November 1929 and became more frequent and violent as the years went by. In 1942, so many employees were on strike that trains could not run. The TP&W was considered a valuable asset to the war effort during World War II, so it was seized from McNear by the government. Striking employees went back to work, but when the railroad was returned to McNear's control after the war, they immediately went on strike again. An incident in February 1946 resulted in two pickets being killed under suspicious circumstances by armed guards McNear had hired. The violent crescendo continued until March 10, 1947, when McNear was suddenly murdered. While suspected to be an angered railroad employee, the assailant was never identified, and to this day the murder of George McNear remains unsolved.

George Plummer McNear Jr. was born on June 15, 1891, in Petaluma, California. After serving in World War I, he moved to New York City, where he became a successful businessman. When he purchased the TP&W in 1926, he moved with his wife and children to Peoria. Following his death in 1947, his family returned to California. (Photograph by Harris & Ewing, courtesy of the Prints and Photographs Division, Library of Congress.)

One of George McNear's improvements to the railroad came in 1927 when four brand new 2-8-2 steam locomotives were purchased. They were built by the American Locomotive Company of Schenectady, New York, and were capable of speeds up to 60 miles per hour. (Photograph by Robert Graham, author's collection.)

TOLEDO, PEORIA & WESTERN RAILROAD

TIME TABLE No. 11

Time Table No. 11

Taking Effect at 12:01 A. M., Dec. 6, 1931

Superseding Time Table No. 10

DESTROY ALL TIME TABLES OF PREVIOUS DATE

This Time Table is for the exclusive use and guidance of the employees concerned, who must carry in addition thereto the book of rules of the operating department.

In 1926, regular passenger train operations began to be eliminated. Increasing competition with automobiles resulted in the TP&W's passenger trains losing money, and George McNear wanted them gone. By the time this 1931 timetable was published, only mixed train service was offered, meaning that a single passenger car was attached to a freight train. Mixed trains were discontinued by the end of the decade. (Author's collection.)

This photograph of passenger car No. 19 was taken in the 1940s. While passenger trains were discontinued in the 1930s, George McNear retained a handful of passenger cars for special trips to inspect the railroad with fellow executives. After McNear's death, most of these passenger cars were scrapped. (Courtesy of the Paul H. Stringham Collection, Special Collections Center, Bradley University Library.)

In 1928, the TP&W opened a new rail yard, repair shop, and locomotive servicing facility at East Peoria, Illinois, just across the Illinois River from Peoria. Previously, the TP&W's shops and yard were located off of Persimmon Street in Peoria. This aerial view shows the new shops in East Peoria. (Courtesy of TP&W Historical Society Collection.)

PEORIA, ILL. MAY 2 5 1937   19   No. 340

CENTRAL HANOVER BANK AND TRUST COMPANY 1-33
SEVENTY BROADWAY

PAY
TO THE
ORDER OF   THE FIRST NATIONAL BANK
OF PEORIA, ILLINOIS $ 50,000.

T.P.&W.R.R. 50000 & 00 CTS. NO PRO,   DOLLARS
70-1

TREASURER   Geo P. McNear   PRESIDENT

This check from 1937 was likely for transferring funds between two official company bank accounts. George McNear was very strict about finances and insisted that every company check had to be hand signed by him, with no exceptions. This check, along with several other historical documents, were rescued from a dumpster in the East Peoria yard in the early 1980s. (Author's collection.)

27

In March 1937, the TP&W received six brand new 4-8-4 type steam locomotives from the American Locomotive Company. The engines, numbered from 80 to 85, were the lightest 4-8-4 locomotives in North America, weighing approximately 361,000 pounds each, as opposed to other 4-8-4 locomotives that weighed over 500,000 pounds. They were designed to pull freight trains at high speeds and were capable of traveling up to 80 miles per hour, but it is unlikely they ever reached that speed. Nicknamed the "80 Class Engines" by TP&W employees, they were the last steam locomotives ever purchased by the TP&W. (Photograph by Robert Graham, author's collection.)

This 1939 photograph shows one of the new 80 class locomotives in downtown Peoria. The stripe running down the middle of the locomotive and coal tender was green with yellow pinstripes, while the rest of the locomotive was gray and black. Originally, the stripe was supposed to be red, but George McNear did not approve of the color and had it changed to green. (Photograph by Robert Graham, author's collection.)

For many years, Leo Clark was the engineer on the TP&W with the highest seniority. He started on the TP&W as a fireman in 1917 after a brief career on the Wabash Railroad. He became an engineer a few years later and held that position until his retirement in 1969. In his spare time, he was a photographer and railroad enthusiast, and began taking his camera to work with him to take pictures of the railroad and the trains he operated. Today, such activities would be forbidden, but during Clark's career, as long as the work got done in a safe, efficient, and timely manner, management did not care about employees taking pictures while on duty. By the time of his death in 1988, Leo Clark had one of the largest TP&W photograph collections in the world. This photograph from September 4, 1941, shows him posing in front of one of the massive wheels of locomotive No. 85. (Courtesy of the Clark/Finson Collection, Special Collections Center, Bradley University Library.)

This photograph from the 1940s shows TP&W brakeman Leon Page (center), with two waitresses on a lunch break at a restaurant in Ferris, Illinois. For many years, TP&W train crews would stop their trains in various towns along the railroad for a few minutes so they could get off, stretch their legs, and get something to eat. In later years, the Dairy Queen in El Paso, Illinois, was a particularly favored stopping point for TP&W crews as it was right next to the tracks. If in a hurry, the crew would call ahead and have a restaurant prepare food for them so they could quickly pick it up upon their arrival. While not as common as they once were, train crews still occasionally make "food break" stops today. (Courtesy of the Clark/Finson Collection, Special Collections Center, Bradley University Library.)

The TP&W operated trains carrying perishable goods for many years. Trains made up of special refrigerated boxcars called "reefers" would be brought to the TP&W by other railroads at Keokuk, Lomax, and Peoria. From there, the TP&W would take them to Effner, Indiana, where they were handed off to the Pennsylvania Railroad for shipment to the east coast. Prior to the implementation of electronic refrigerator units on reefer cars, large blocks of ice were loaded into the cars to keep the goods cool. The TP&W owned and operated an icing station for this purpose at East Peoria. This photograph from the early 1940s shows a perishable goods train preparing to leave Keokuk for Effner, where the train was handed over to the Pennsylvania Railroad. (Courtesy of the Keokuk Public Library.)

For much of the steam locomotive era on US railroads during the 19th and 20th centuries, several of these structures could be found along any railroad. Toward the end of the 1800s, steam locomotives began burning coal instead of wood. The large tower on the left was filled with coal, and locomotives that were running low on fuel could stop underneath and have their supply replenished. The water tower served the same purpose, but for water, which was used to make steam. The TP&W had water and coaling towers at many locations, including Watseka, Forrest, Chenoa, Gridley, Eureka, East Peoria, Hollis, Glasford, Cuba, Bushnell, La Harpe, and Warsaw. As locomotive technology advanced, larger locomotives with larger tenders for storing fuel and water were introduced, and the need for frequent stops decreased. This photograph, taken in the 1930s, shows the coaling and water facilities in Cuba, Illinois. (Courtesy of the Clark/Finson Collection, Special Collections Center, Bradley University Library.)

Locomotive No. 83 is heading west through the small village of La Hogue, Illinois, just west of Gilman, on its way to Peoria. For many years, La Hogue was pronounced "La Hog" by train crews. When the 80 class locomotives were retired and scrapped in the 1950s, several pieces from them were saved and survive today in private collections around the country. (Photograph by Robert Graham, author's collection.)

Prior to 1940, the TP&W identified its cabooses by letters instead of numbers like most railroads. Caboose K was originally built in the 1890s, but by the time this photograph was taken in the 1940s, it had been extensively rebuilt and modified several times. (Courtesy of the Paul H. Stringham Collection, Special Collections Center, Bradley University Library.)

On June 19, 1940, the first numbered caboose on the TP&W, No. 201, entered service. Built by the TP&W's own East Peoria shops instead of a railcar manufacturer, the 201 was the first of six numbered cabooses built that year. The other five, Nos. 202, 203, 204, 205, and 206, were all built and entered service during the following months, with the final caboose entering service in October. Eventually, the older, lettered cabooses received numbers as well to avoid confusion. In 1948, the 200-series cabooses were renumbered into the 500s as the railroad had purchased new locomotives that had the 200-series numbers. No. 201 became the 501, the 202 became the 502, and so on. This photograph shows the 201/501 after it had been renumbered. Over time, these cabooses became known as the "McNear Cabooses." (Photograph by the author.)

This photograph from the early 1940s shows brakeman Leon Page inside Caboose 205 filling out paperwork. Cabooses served as mobile offices for train crews and often featured desks, chairs, restrooms, and stoves. No. 205 was later renumbered to 505 and survives today on private property in Lacon, Illinois. (Courtesy of the Clark/Finson Collection, Special Collections Center, Bradley University Library.)

This poster was used to inform union members of a planned strike against the TP&W. George McNear, as one employee once said, was a "labor hater." He ordered any worker caught attending a union meeting to be fired. For many employees, losing their job during the Great Depression was not an option. As a result, most union meetings were held secretly. (Photograph by the author.)

This photograph, likely from the 1930s, shows George McNear (standing sixth from left) and his fellow railroad executives posing on a passenger car for a group photograph. Many of the other men shown here were also strict and harsh with lower-ranking TP&W employees. Some people have said that they went as far as to enforce a limit to the amount of toilet tissue people could use in the company offices. Anyone who spoke up about these conditions was quickly fired. After many years of strikes that often resulted in all railroad operations being halted, McNear had had enough and hired non-union employees to run his trains while the strikes went on. At one point, McNear himself climbed aboard a switch engine at the East Peoria yard and began switching cars to show the strikers that he did not need them. These conflicts resulted in the creation and development of national labor laws and unions that are still in place today. (Courtesy of Dean Cunningham.)

On February 6, 1946, engineer Arthur Browne and agent Irwin Paschon, two striking employees who were blocking a train at Gridley, Illinois, with other pickets, were killed by armed guards who George McNear had hired to protect his trains. The guards were charged with murder and tried at the McLean County Courthouse in Bloomington, Illinois. They claimed that they had fired in self-defense, and were eventually acquitted. After this incident, the strikes continued to get worse. A little over a year later on March 10, 1947, George McNear was killed by an unknown assailant while walking home from a Bradley University basketball game in Peoria. While suspected to be the work of an angry employee, his murder remains unsolved. The day after his death, some employees walked into the company office building to meet with executives. The executives, frightened for their safety, asked, "What was it that you wanted again?" This photograph shows McNear's home in Peoria. (Photograph by the author.)

Four

THE COULTER ERA

On May 1, 1947, John Russel "Russ" Coulter was appointed president of the Toledo, Peoria & Western, replacing George McNear. Similar to his late predecessor, Coulter quickly and aggressively went to work improving the railroad. As early as the late 1940s, he began making a serious effort to improve public and employee relations with the company, as they had been damaged during the conflicts when McNear was president. By the early 1950s, the TP&W was hosting a radio show in Peoria, and each summer held an awards ceremony at its headquarters building for the public. At these ceremonies, Coulter and other TP&W executives presented awards to employees or people from towns along the railroad who went above and beyond to support either the railroad or their community. Coulter also did many things to improve the railroad physically. One of these improvements was made in December 1947, when the TP&W received its first set of modern diesel locomotives. Coulter and other managers quickly recognized the success of this new type of locomotive, and in 1950, the TP&W had become one of the first railroads in the country to completely "dieselize" its fleet. In 1960, the Pennsylvania Railroad and the Santa Fe Railway acquired joint ownership of the TP&W, but the railroad continued to operate as an independent company. Thanks to Coulter's business tactics, the TP&W was once again able to survive troubling times and prospered through the 1950s and 1960s.

George McNear left behind a number of things on the TP&W, the largest of which was this Pullman observation car that he had purchased to travel around the property. It was built in 1890 as a private car for millionaire John Bunting, a brakeman for the Southern Pacific Railroad who made a fortune in the oil industry. After being sold to several different companies throughout the early 1900s, it finally wound up on the TP&W in 1926. Following McNear's murder in 1947, it was parked on a sidetrack in East Peoria until 1957. This photograph shows the car in storage at East Peoria in April 1949. (Author's collection.)

This photograph from October 2, 1950, shows one of the TP&W's troop sleeper cars at Canton, Illinois. Built by the Pullman Company during World War II, they were used as sleeping cars on military trains transporting soldiers. After the war, they were sold and repurposed. The TP&W's were turned into bunkhouses for maintenance crews. (Photograph by Merle Graves, courtesy of John Stell.)

By 1950, the process of replacing steam locomotives with diesels on the TP&W was in full swing. Unfortunately, during this time, little was being done to preserve historic railroad equipment. As a result, all of the TP&W's steam locomotives were scrapped. This 1949 photograph shows locomotive No. 71 awaiting shipment to the scrap yard. (Photograph by Paul H. Stringham, author's collection.)

In December 1947, the TP&W purchased its first diesel locomotives from the Electro-Motive Division (EMD) of General Motors in LaGrange, Illinois. They had been used for demonstrations by EMD prior to the purchase, so they received a TP&W paint job before being shipped to Peoria. The two locomotives were nicknamed "Bertha" and "Beulah" by TP&W employees. (Photograph by the EMD Company, author's collection.)

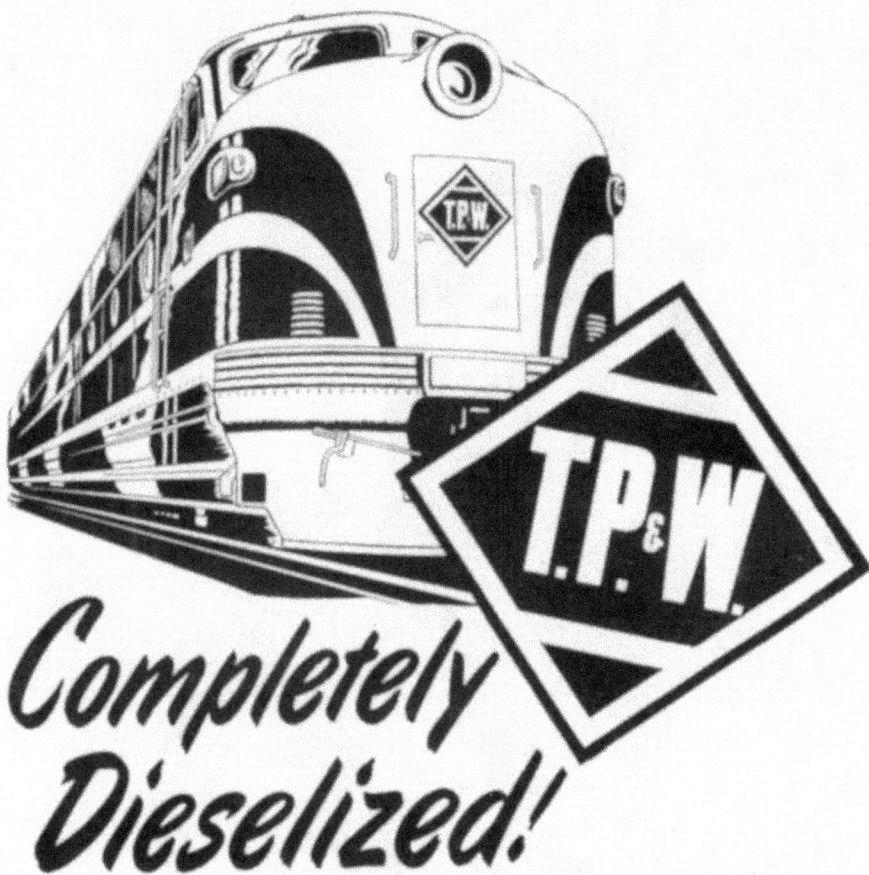

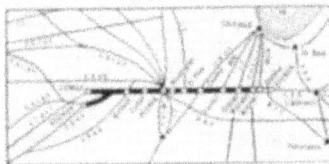

On October 11, 1950, the final steam train ran on the TP&W. Shortly after the last steam engines were hauled off to the scrapyard, this advertisement was published by the TP&W management, proudly stating that the railroad was now "completely dieselized." It was one of the first railroads to achieve this, as most others continued using steam into the late 1950s. (Author's collection.)

One of Russ Coulter's public relations tools was Tee Pee Willie, the official mascot of the TP&W. Willie was first introduced in the early 1950s and made many appearances on advertisements and company merchandise. He served as the railroad's mascot for 30 years. (Author's collection.)

Montague L. "Monty" Powell started his railroad career at age 14 in 1942 as a telegrapher for the Illinois Central. At the time, he was the youngest railroad employee in the country and was featured in multiple newspaper articles. In 1947, he went to work for the TP&W as an interlocking tower operator. In 1952, he became a dispatcher. For several years, he worked at the Walnut Street Tower in Peoria, where he and other operators directed train movements over a junction between the TP&W and Rock Island Railroad. Powell retired in 1989. He was a lifelong railroad fan and photographer and took thousands of photographs of trains in the Peoria area both during his career and after his retirement. (Courtesy of John Stell.)

The Honegger Feed Company was founded in 1928 by Samuel and Frank Honegger, two brothers from Forrest, Illinois. They produced high-quality livestock feed and had a very successful business during the 1930s, 1940s, and 1950s. On February 24, 1949, their feed mill in downtown Fairbury, Illinois, burned to the ground. Soon after, the construction of a new facility began on the west side of Fairbury. Opened on August 3, 1950, the new feed mill was fully automated. A single operator could control the process of making the feed and packaging it from a control room overlooking the operation. The new facility was served by both the TP&W and Wabash Railroads, which delivered empty hopper cars for transporting feed and picked them up after they were filled. The feed mill closed on June 30, 1989; today, only the silos remain. (Author's collection.)

This photograph from the early 1950s shows diesel locomotive No. 101 passing through La Harpe, Illinois, with a short freight train. The 101 was one of the first two diesel locomotives acquired by the TP&W in 1947. Originally numbered 100B, the locomotive was a "B unit," meaning that it had no cab or controls for the engineer. Instead, it was connected with locomotive 100, which was an "A unit" and had a special setup where the engineer could control both locomotives from the cab of the 100. The TP&W realized that if the 100 was out of service for repairs or maintenance, the 100B could not operate either. To fix this issue, through the efforts of the railroad's shop forces, the 100B was rebuilt into an A unit. It emerged from the shop in January 1950 as No. 101 and operated that way until it was retired in the early 1960s. When completed, the 101 was three inches shorter than the nearly-identical 100. (Photograph by Dick Abner, courtesy of Thomas Waldon.)

As mentioned in the previous chapter, in 1940, the TP&W built a fleet of six new cabooses. Beginning in the early 1950s, additional cabooses were built at the East Peoria shops. This 1956 photograph shows a line of newly-built cabooses outside of the shops awaiting paint and final preparations before being placed into service. (Courtesy of the Paul H. Stringham Collection, Special Collections Center, Bradley University Library.)

Caboose No. 508, pictured here at the East Peoria yard on August 28, 1958, was originally built in 1888 as a wooden caboose with a cupola. Over the following decades, the car was rebuilt several times. It is very likely that nothing from the original 1888 construction survived at the time of this photograph. (Photograph by Montague L. Powell, courtesy of John Stell.)

TREAT YOURSELF TO ENJOYMENT...

hear "SINGING RAILS"

over W M B D

1470 ON YOUR DIAL

EVERY SUNDAY AT 4:00 P.M.

A Program of Outstanding Music
Brought To You By

The Toledo, Peoria & Western Railroad

During the late 1950s and early 1960s, the TP&W hosted a Sunday radio show on the WMBD station in Peoria. The show played hit songs of the time and recognized various people who had either supported the TP&W-served community or the railroad directly. (Courtesy of Harold Krewer.)

For many years, Effner, Indiana, was the east end of the line for TP&W trains. East of the Effner depot, pictured here, the tracks were owned by the Pennsylvania Railroad. Locomotives were turned to return westward at Effner on a special track called a "Wye," which was a Y-shaped track that allowed trains to make a three-point turn. The Wye track was owned by the Pennsylvania Railroad, which charged the TP&W $1 per turn to use it. At one time, in addition to the station, Effner also had a small locomotive servicing facility (see page 21) and a boardinghouse for train crews to spend the night in. The servicing facility was removed before World War II, but the boardinghouse remained. During the 1950s, Russ Coulter set up a museum in the boardinghouse called the TeePee. The museum featured many displays of historical railroad artifacts that had been stored in the company archives in Peoria. (Photograph by Roger A. Holmes.)

Farmdale, Illinois, is a junction on the TP&W just east of the East Peoria yard. At Farmdale, the TP&W crossed the Nickel Plate Road (now Norfolk Southern Railway) and a now-abandoned branch line of the Pennsylvania Railroad. Prior to 1950, the tracks at Farmdale crossed each other at the same level on a special piece of track called a "diamond." However, frequent flooding in the area from the nearby Illinois River was becoming an increasing concern, so in the late 1940s, planning began for a new reservoir at Farmdale. The project required the relocation and elevation of the TP&W line. When completed, the TP&W crossed the Nickel Plate on a bridge instead of a diamond. The reservoir and track relocation were completed in 1950, and the old Farmdale diamond and a nearby depot and interlocking tower were removed. This photograph shows the Farmdale bridge over the former Nickel Plate Road tracks. (Photograph by the author.)

FORM 19 | **TOLEDO, PEORIA & WESTERN RAILROAD** | **FORM 19**

Train Order No. 1

PEORIA, ILL. July 23, 1950

To All Eastward Trains | At Farmdale

X _____ Opr. _____ M.

Reduce to 20 Miles Per Hour

Mile Post 78-15 to 78-32

10 Miles Per Hour Mile Post

90-32 to 91-10

H.H.B.

Superintendent

EACH EMPLOYE ADDRESSED MUST HAVE A COPY OF THIS ORDER

MADE	TIME	DISPATCHER	OPERATOR
Com	1212A M	D.S.21.	Powell

Prior to the implementation of computers and radios in the railroad industry, a common type of paperwork used was a train order form. These documents were filled out by operators at depots and interlocking towers and given to crews on passing trains. They informed the train crews of just about anything they needed to know, whether it was a notification that they would be passing another train a few miles ahead or if they had to drop off or pick up cars somewhere. Most railroads' train orders were on very thin paper, which earned them the nickname "flimsies." Paper copies of train orders were largely phased out beginning in the 1980s. This one, signed by operator Monty Powell on July 23, 1950, was the last train order ever signed at the Farmdale interlocking tower before it was closed and the TP&W's tracks were rerouted for the reservoir. (Author's collection.)

In September 1959, the New York Central Railroad, which crossed the TP&W at Sheldon, Illinois, displayed its historic steam locomotive No. 999 on the TP&W's track in town. No. 999 was built in 1893 to pull passenger trains to and from the World's Fair in Chicago. While there is no official record, it is said that it was the first locomotive to reach 100 miles per hour. The New York Central recognized its significance, and proudly maintained and ran it around its system during the first half of the 20th century for display in various communities. Following a management change on the New York Central, No. 999 was retired and destined for the scrap yard. However, it was later saved and preserved. Today, the locomotive is displayed at the Museum of Science and Industry in Chicago. (Courtesy of the Clark/Finson Collection, Special Collections Center, Bradley University Library.)

In 1949, the TP&W's management purchased this Pullman passenger car for use as a business car for railroad executives to travel around the property. The passenger cars used for this purpose by George McNear and his executives had either been scrapped or sold by this time. The new car was named the *Prairie Marksman*, paying homage to a high-priority TP&W freight train of the late 1800s that carried the same name. In 1956, the need for an additional business car arose, but instead of purchasing another passenger car, the management instructed the East Peoria shops to build a caboose specially designed for use as a business car. Once completed, the special caboose became the *Prairie Marksman II*. Beginning in the late 1950s, the two cars began to be chartered by local railroad clubs for special excursion trips over the TP&W for railroad fans. This continued until about 1965, when the *Prairie Marksman* was sold to a private owner in Virginia, and the *Prairie Marksman II* was converted to a regular caboose. (Author's collection.)

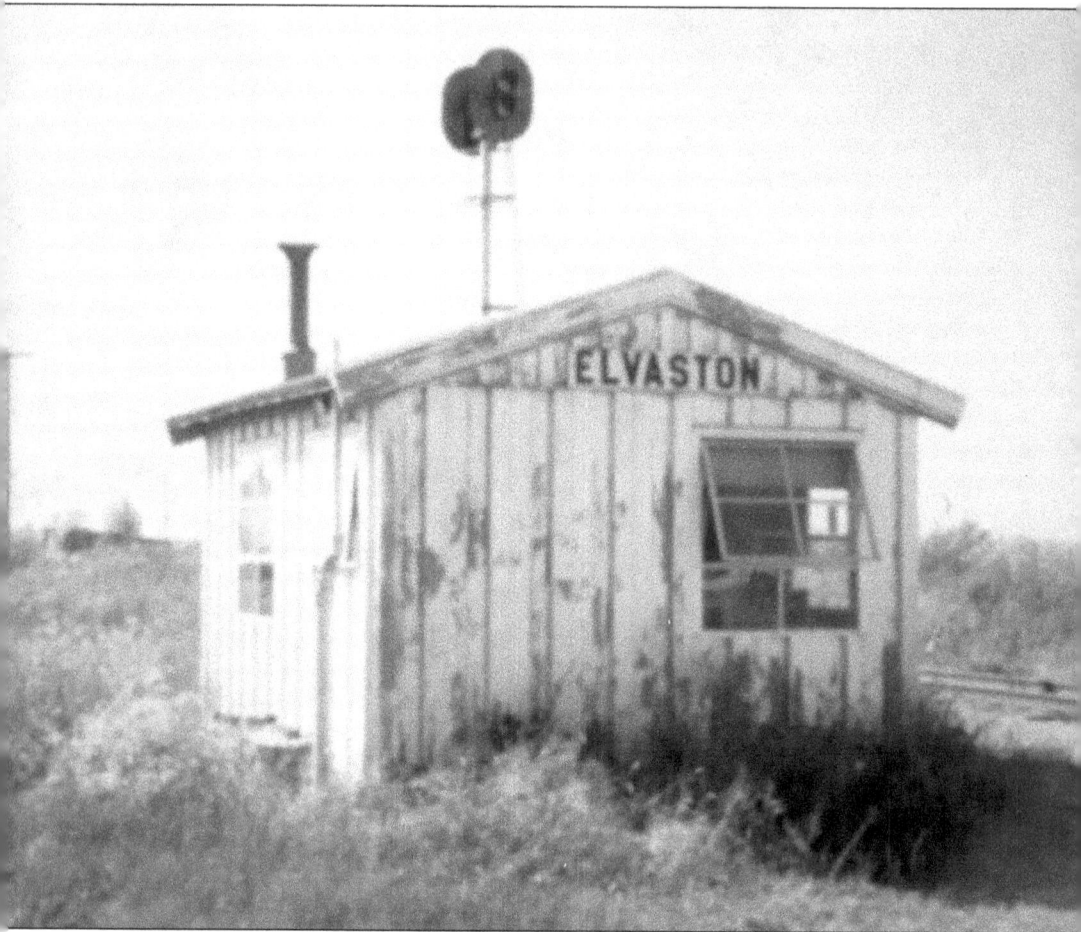

In the early 1960s, the TP&W demolished several older station buildings in various towns along the railroad and replaced them with newer, smaller, less-attractive metal structures. The older stations were much larger than the new ones, and due to the discontinuance of passenger trains during the George McNear presidency, the need for buildings of their size diminished. However, with continuing freight business and the occasional passenger who was allowed to purchase a ticket and ride in the caboose of a freight train, there was still a need for depots along the TP&W. This new station was built at Elvaston, Illinois, in 1962. (Photograph by John Stell.)

On June 20, 1951, the TP&W opened this new company headquarters building near the East Peoria yard. This building had lots of office space, which allowed for the relocation of several jobs that were formerly located inside of the Peoria Union Depot and other facilities. This building still stands today, though it is no longer owned by the railroad. (Photograph by Bernie Smith, author's collection.)

In 1963, the TP&W sent its first diesel locomotive, No. 100 (see page 42), to the General Motors locomotive factory to be stripped of parts and scrapped. The parts salvaged were used to construct this locomotive, a GP30 type diesel, which was completed in September 1963 and sent to the TP&W. The 700 was the TP&W's only GP30 locomotive. (Photograph by Robert Stevens, author's collection.)

This photograph from June 1968 shows RS3 diesel locomotive No. 207 leading a short freight train out of the East Peoria yard. An overpass for Route 150 is in the background. No. 207 was built in December 1950 and scrapped in May 1983. (Photograph by Rick Burn.)

In January 1952, the TP&W acquired these two identical GP7 type locomotives from General Motors. Numbered 102 and 103, the two locomotives worked on the TP&W until 1983, when they were sold to the Michigan Northern Railroad. This photograph shows them in Canton, Illinois. (Photograph by John Stell.)

This RS2 type locomotive was built by the American Locomotive Company in Schenectady, New York, in September 1949. The TP&W owned seven RS2 locomotives, numbered 200 through 206. Most were scrapped in the 1960s and 1970s, but No. 205 and No. 202 were used until 1983, when they were sold to the Octoraro Railroad in Pennsylvania. (Courtesy of John and Roger Kujawa.)

In 1965, the Toledo, Peoria & Western (TP&W) acquired three GP35 type locomotives from General Motors. These new engines were numbered 900, 901, and 902. When they were delivered to the TP&W in November of that year, they were the most powerful locomotives on the railroad. The individual engines were capable of generating 2,500 horsepower. (Photograph by Rick Burn.)

The TP&W purchased three RS11 type locomotives from the American Locomotive Company in the late 1950s. Nos. 400 and 401 were built in November 1958, while No. 402 was built in June 1959. No. 400 was known as a "class unit," the first locomotive of its type on the railroad. (Photograph by Montague L. Powell, courtesy of John Stell.)

This photograph from July 1962 shows locomotive No. 401 leading a westbound freight train across Spring Creek west of Crescent City, Illinois. This location was once known as Leonard, and at the beginning of the 20th century, a depot was located here. Today, it is just a few houses and the railroad tracks. (Photograph by Rick Burn.)

This photograph from 1962 shows a westbound freight train at Gilman, Illinois, with locomotive 401 in the lead. The train is about to cross the north-south Illinois Central Railroad, whose tracks can be seen in the foreground. To the right are the roof overhangs of the TP&W's Gilman freight depot, which was built in 1877. (Photograph by Rick Burn.)

No. 401 was originally identical to No. 400, but following extensive damage from an August 28, 1964, wreck near Cuba, Illinois, it was rebuilt with a "chop nose," meaning that the front of the locomotive was shortened in height. This allowed better visibility for the train crew. This photograph shows No. 401 and No. 400 at the East Peoria yard. (Photograph by Harold Krewer.)

In 1964, the TP&W purchased two new C424 type diesel locomotives from the American Locomotive Company. Numbered 800 and 801, the locomotives ran on the TP&W until early 1983, when they were both sold to the Morristown & Erie Railroad in New Jersey. (Author's collection.)

The TP&W utilized a small fleet of rebuilt passenger cars for maintenance service. Car No. 126, pictured here, was built by the Pullman Company as a mail car for handling long-distance mail shipments. By the time this photograph was taken in the East Peoria yard, it had been rebuilt to house maintenance crews and material. (Author's collection.)

Five

THE FINAL YEARS

After several prosperous years during the postwar period of the 1950s and 1960s, the good times on the Toledo, Peoria & Western once again came to an end. The 1970s were difficult for many railroads around the country, and the TP&W was no exception. Trouble began on February 12, 1970, when a barge struck the railroad's bridge over the Illinois River at Peoria. Unable to afford a new bridge, the TP&W was forced to negotiate with the Peoria & Pekin Union Railway for trackage rights over another bridge nearby. Later that year on June 21, a train derailed at Crescent City, Illinois, and hazardous materials that were being transported on the train ignited and exploded, destroying much of the downtown area. The lawsuits from the Crescent City wreck and the expensive trackage rights proved to be an extreme financial challenge for the railroad. To make matters worse, mergers and company changes of railroads that connected to the TP&W in the 1970s, along with overall declining rail business, hurt the TP&W's revenues. On July 20, 1979, the Santa Fe Railway, which connected to the TP&W at Lomax, Illinois, purchased a controlling interest in the company. The TP&W became an official subsidiary of the Santa Fe on March 1, 1981. It continued to operate independently until January 1, 1984, when it was merged into the Santa Fe as a whole, ending a 135-year history.

In 1968, four SW1500 type switcher locomotives were purchased. They were painted in a new red-orange and white color scheme. The railroad executives liked this new look, and by the 1970s, other TP&W locomotives were being repainted to match the switchers. By 1980, only a couple of locomotives were still in the old green and yellow paint of the 1950s and 1960s. (Photograph by Larry Anglund, author's collection.)

In 1969, the TP&W acquired its only GP40 type diesel locomotive, No. 1000. Built by the Electro-Motive Division of General Motors, the 1000 was originally used by EMD for demonstrations before coming to the TP&W. It arrived on the property in black paint and operated that way until it was eventually repainted into TP&W colors. (Photograph by Montague L. Powell, courtesy of John Stell.)

This photograph from February 1970 shows the TP&W's bridge over the Illinois River at Peoria after it had been struck by a barge. After this accident, railroad management decided to establish a trackage rights agreement over the Peoria & Pekin Union Railway (P&PU), which had a bridge of its own south of the TP&W's bridge. (Courtesy of the Paul H. Stringham Collection, Special Collections Center, Bradley University Library.)

This photograph shows a westbound freight train crossing the P&PU bridge on the south side of Peoria. Following the 1970 barge accident, TP&W trains began using the P&PU's bridge instead. TP&W trains still use this bridge today. (Photograph by Harold Krewer.)

On Father's Day, June 21, 1970, an overheated hopper car wheel bearing on eastbound freight train No. 20 caused a derailment in downtown Crescent City, Illinois. Several tank cars that derailed were carrying liquid propane. One of the tank cars was punctured, and the propane ignited. The blaze quickly spread to the other cars with propane, and the subsequent fires and explosions completely destroyed much of the downtown area of Crescent City. The force of the explosions sent chunks of freight cars hundreds of feet into the air, and to this day, small bits of them can still be found in farm fields surrounding the town. The final fire from the wreck burned out on June 23, and soon after, the rebuilding process began. Originally, the town planned to rebuild every building that was lost, but in the end, only a few were replaced. Playgrounds, basketball and tennis courts, and parking lots now stand where buildings used to be, serving as eerie reminders of the wreck. (Courtesy of Matt Smith.)

This photograph is a good example of how powerful the explosions from the wreck were. Chunks of freight cars became projectiles and caused significant damage around the wreck site. This part of a tank car landed in someone's living room. Miraculously, while there were some injuries, no lives were lost in the entire event. (Courtesy of Matt Smith.)

In the wake of the Crescent City wreck, the town rebuilt and firefighters around the country learned from the wreck to be better prepared for any future events of a similar nature. A small memorial was erected at the site of the wreck in downtown Crescent City. Parts of destroyed railcars, photographs, and old newspapers are displayed there. (Photograph by the author.)

In 1959, the TP&W built the Kolbe Industrial Spur, a small branch line that split off from the main line just north of Mapleton, Illinois, to access various industries along the Illinois River. A small depot was built at the point where the spur left the main line. John Stell, who worked at the Kolbe depot from 1968 to 1976, shared an interesting story from his time working there. One day, a freight train was passing the depot, and he spotted a boxcar that had somehow caught fire. He alerted the train crew and together they decided to stop the train a few miles away at Glasford, where there was a fire station near the tracks. He called the fire department and they prepared for the train's arrival. It was quickly discovered that the car was filled with new rolls of toilet tissue, which quickly burned once the fire had started. The Glasford Fire Department later told Stell that it was the first time someone had brought a fire to them. (Photograph by the author.)

In 1968, the TP&W acquired two cabooses secondhand from the Santa Fe Railway. Numbered 529 and 530, once repainted into TP&W colors, the two cabooses were used on freight trains until 1983, when they were both sold to railroad fans for preservation. Caboose 530, pictured here, was damaged in a fire in the late 1970s, and the raised cupola was removed during the repair process. (Author's collection.)

During the bicentennial celebrations in America in 1975 and 1976, several railroads selected single locomotives to paint into a special red, white, and blue color scheme. The TP&W selected locomotive No. 700, and it was repainted in 1975. (Photograph by Robert Stevens, author's collection.)

In 1968, the Pennsylvania Railroad, which connected to the TP&W at Effner, merged with the New York Central Railroad to form Penn Central. Penn Central began struggling financially early on, and in 1976, it was merged into the Consolidated Rail Corporation (Conrail). Conrail decided that the former Pennsylvania line that went to Effner from Kenneth, Indiana, just outside of Logansport, was unnecessary for its system, so it was sold to the TP&W on April 1, 1976. The TP&W now had track from the Mississippi River all the way to central Indiana, the most it had ever owned. This photograph shows some TP&W locomotives at the village of Remington, Indiana, on the former Pennsylvania line to Logansport. The grain elevator in the background still stands today and is still served by trains. (Author's collection.)

In order to eliminate the need to swap locomotives at the end of the line, the TP&W and Penn Central decided to leave their locomotives on trains that they were handing off to each other. As a result, Penn Central locomotives ran on TP&W trains and vice-versa. This photograph shows a TP&W train with Penn Central locomotives at Bushnell, Illinois. Engineer Blache Barnett is on the left. (Courtesy of Jason Jordan.)

A westbound Penn Central freight train with Penn Central locomotive No. 2720 passes the Kolbe depot north of Mapleton, Illinois. No. 2720, a U23B type locomotive, was built by General Electric in August 1972. After the Penn Central shut down in 1976, it became Conrail No. 2720 and was retired and scrapped in 1993. (Courtesy of John and Roger Kujawa.)

For a couple of years in the late 1970s, locomotives 202 and 205 were used together on the Kolbe Local, a train that traveled from the East Peoria yard to the Kolbe Industrial Spur to pick up and drop off freight cars at industries. This photograph shows the train passing through an industrial area south of Peoria. (Photograph by Roger A. Holmes.)

In 1977, Robert E. McMillan became the final president of the TP&W before it was merged into the Santa Fe Railway in 1984. McMillan had an extensive railroading career, beginning in 1941 as a maintenance worker on the Illinois Central. He retired in April 1984 and passed away in 2013. (Photograph by Dave Arganbright.)

On June 1, 1977, the TP&W received four new diesel locomotives from the Electro-Motive Division of General Motors. Designated class GP38-2, the railroad would eventually order seven more of these locomotives in 1978. These were the last locomotives acquired before the TP&W was merged into the Santa Fe Railway. (Author's collection.)

Larry Fraikes was one of the dispatchers on the TP&W who controlled train movements over the entire railroad. Dispatchers were based in East Peoria and communicated with trains all over the system via radio. This photograph shows Fraikes at work in the dispatcher office. (Photograph by Roger A. Holmes.)

Sperry Rail Service was founded in 1928 by Elmer Sperry. The company contracts with various railroads, using special self-propelled railcars with instruments that inspect the tracks for defects. This photograph shows one of the Sperry inspection cars at the East Peoria yard after dark. (Photograph by Harold Krewer.)

Throughout its history, the TP&W had many interesting pieces of maintenance equipment. This photograph, taken at Cuba, Illinois, shows the TP&W's brush cutter vehicle, which traveled along the tracks and removed brush that was growing near them. This vehicle was later destroyed after being accidentally struck by a freight train. (Photograph by John Stell.)

Diesel locomotive No. 900 is on the turntable at East Peoria. Turntables were used to turn locomotives around, mainly during the steam era, and were largely phased out when diesel locomotives took over. However, the one installed at the East Peoria yard remained in service for decades after the last steam locomotive used it. (Photograph by Robert Stevens, author's collection.)

On July 27, 1975, locomotive 402 made its final run. It was placed into storage at the East Peoria yard until January 1978, when it was moved inside the shop and rebuilt into a special snow plow car. The locomotive parts were removed and the interior was filled with concrete for extra weight to assist with plowing. (Courtesy of Jason Jordan.)

This photograph from May 19, 1976, shows the Toledo, Peoria & Western's yard office building at the East Peoria yard. Inside were offices for dispatchers, supervisors, mechanics, and clerks. This building was torn down in the 1980s after the Santa Fe Railway took over the property. (Photograph by John Stell.)

Two TP&W hopper cars are at Logansport, Indiana, in August 1977, just over a year after the tracks from Effner to Logansport were acquired by the TP&W. These cars were built by the Pullman-Standard Company. (Bruce Emmons Collection, courtesy of Jason Jordan.)

Crane car No. 99 was used for lifting heavy objects along the railroad and was occasionally used to assist with clearing derailments. This photograph from September 1981 shows the crane on a maintenance train at Effner. (Photograph by Bruce Emmons, courtesy of Jason Jordan.)

Soon after the TP&W acquired track into Logansport in 1976, the railroad's bright red-orange and white locomotives became a common sight in town. This photograph shows locomotive 2005 in front of a former Pennsylvania Railroad freight depot left over from the previous owners of the line. (Photograph by Roger A. Holmes.)

A train crew poses in front of an SW1500 type switcher locomotive at the East Peoria yard. From left to right are David Plotts, Gene Conners, Bill Marshall, and Don Lucas. (Photograph by Leo Clark, courtesy of John Stell.)

This 1975 photograph shows switchman Vern Oesch onboard switcher locomotive No. 303 at East Peoria. The train is organizing freight cars in the yard on different tracks. The cars it is switching are gondolas, which were used for carrying low-priority items such as scrap metal or rock. (Photograph by Robert Stevens, author's collection.)

Locomotive No. 2010 is seen here after dark at the East Peoria yard. After signing a liability release form, photographers were welcome to go anywhere in the yard to photograph trains at all hours of the day. Today, such activities are strictly prohibited on almost all railroads. (Photograph by Roger A. Holmes.)

ConRail gets you to the gate. T.P&W. gets you through it.

There's never been a change in American railroads like ConRail. And, it's working.
But one thing hasn't changed. T. P. & W. is still the fast way across Illinois, providing a delay-free East-West gateway that by-passes big city rail yards.
Can you specify ConRail and T. P. & W.? You bet. We recently purchased 60 miles of right-of-way to link T. P. & W. with ConRail at Logansport, Indiana. Improvements to this line have already begun. We're making a big investment in better service for you.
Specify T. P. & W.

tpw

TOLEDO, PEORIA & WESTERN RAILROAD COMPANY
Home Offices: East Peoria, Illinois

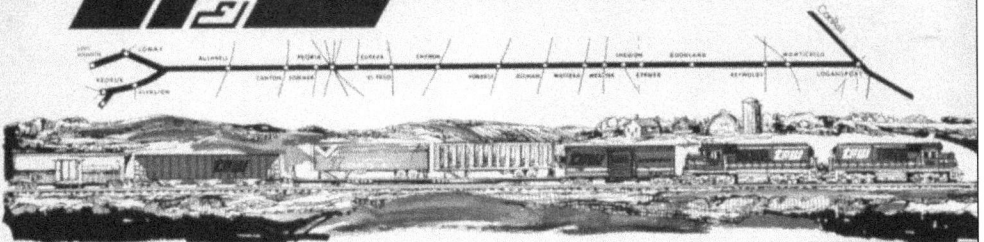

This advertisement published in the late 1970s touts freight service between Logansport and points west. For much of its existence, the TP&W proudly advertised its quick route across Illinois that avoided the often-congested Chicago rail network. (Author's collection.)

In September 1979, Golden Arrow Tours, a private railcar owner and operator, operated a special excursion trip for railroad buffs over the TP&W. Locomotive No. 700 was selected to pull the train and received a fresh paint job prior to the trip. Golden Arrow Tours was not doing too well financially at the time, and could not afford to pay fees to store two of its passenger cars on the TP&W after the trip. Railroad president Robert McMillan held the two cars "captive" until Golden Arrow paid the money owed. It is unknown what eventually became of them, but the two cars were off the property by the end of 1981. This photograph shows the 1979 excursion train passing through the tiny hamlet of Scottsburg, Illinois, near Bushnell. (Photograph by John Stell.)

Less than a year after the Golden Arrow excursion ran, the TP&W generously allowed members of the Fort Wayne Railroad Historical Society of New Haven, Indiana, to bring their newly-restored Nickel Plate Road steam locomotive No. 765 to the TP&W for a series of break-in runs and excursion trips for railroad buffs. For several days in May 1980, the 765 was used to power freight trains east of Peoria and also pulled two passenger excursion trips—one from East Peoria to Effner and return, and one from East Peoria to Keokuk and return. On the trip to Keokuk, the 765 had to be removed from the train at La Harpe, Illinois, due to the track condition between La Harpe and Keokuk not being able to handle its weight. Diesels pulled the train from La Harpe to Keokuk and back to La Harpe, where the 765 took over once again for the return trip to East Peoria. (Photograph by John Stell.)

This photograph from the May 1980 steam locomotive excursion to Keokuk shows a group of railfans waiting for the train on the station platform at Keokuk. Steam locomotives were last seen on the TP&W almost 30 years before this event, so hundreds of people showed up to experience the rare occasion. (Photograph by Harold Krewer.)

In between runs on the TP&W, No. 765 was parked at the East Peoria yards where it was serviced by members of its owner, the Fort Wayne Railroad Historical Society, and TP&W employees. Several TP&W employees who had worked on steam locomotives years before were thrilled to have the 765 visit the railroad for a trip down memory lane. (Photograph by Roger A. Holmes.)

In 1981, the TP&W became a subsidiary of the Santa Fe Railway. The TP&W developed a new logo that was very similar to that of the Santa Fe. It was applied to some equipment before the Santa Fe's management discovered it and ordered it to be removed because it infringed on the Santa Fe's rights. (Courtesy of the Paul H. Stringham Collection, Special Collections Center, Bradley University Library.)

In 1979, a group from the US Department of Transportation visited the TP&W in two inspection cars. They were touring and inspecting the TP&W prior to the inauguration of an Amtrak train that was to traverse the railroad between Chenoa and East Peoria. (Photograph by John Stell.)

Regular passenger train service briefly returned to the TP&W in 1980 and 1981. Through the efforts of TP&W president Robert McMillan and several other Peoria-area businessmen and politicians, on August 10, 1981, Amtrak began the operation of trains 311, 312, and 314, the Prairie Marksman, from Chicago to East Peoria and return. The trains traveled down the former Chicago & Alton Railroad from Chicago to Chenoa, where they used a connection track to get on the TP&W to reach East Peoria. Initially, there was only one intermediate stop between Chicago and East Peoria at Joliet, Illinois, on the former Chicago & Alton route. This changed in early 1981 when an additional stop was added at Eureka, Illinois, along the TP&W. Unfortunately, the Prairie Marksman did not transport enough passengers in 1980 and 1981 to justify its continuance. It made its last run on October 4, 1981, once again ending passenger service on the TP&W. (Photograph by Gene V. Glendinning, courtesy of Dave Arganbright.)

One of the last great achievements of the TP&W before the end of operations in 1984 was the construction of Hoosierlift, a $7.1 million, 31-acre trailer on flat car (TOFC) terminal just outside of Remington, Indiana, on the former Pennsylvania Railroad line to Logansport that the TP&W had acquired in 1976. Hoosierlift was a facility where semi-trailers were loaded and unloaded from railroad flat cars. It was conveniently located just east of Interstate 65, which allowed quick and easy access for truckers. Once the trailers were loaded onto flat cars, the TP&W took them to Lomax, Illinois, where they were handed over to the Santa Fe for shipment to the west coast. Hoosierlift opened in 1983, and while there are no longer any semi-trailers being handled there, it remains an active rail yard today. This photograph shows the massive crane at Hoosierlift used to load trailers onto trains. (Photograph by Bruce Emmons, courtesy of Jason Jordan.)

Another addition to the TP&W during the early 1980s was a group of defect detectors. These trackside machines scanned trains for any issues as they passed. Once the train had cleared the detector, it would broadcast a message over the radio to the crew of the train and provide information about the train and any problems it detected. (Photograph by the author.)

In the early 1980s, new federal regulations required all cabooses to have a special glazing on their windows. The TP&W's management decided it would be cheaper to lease some cabooses owned by the Santa Fe that had the glazing instead of upgrading their own. This photograph shows two leased cabooses at Gilman, Illinois. (Photograph by Bruce Emmons, courtesy of Jason Jordan.)

This photograph from May 1983 shows a freight train at El Paso, Illinois. This train was a "local" bound for Effner, meaning it stopped in several towns along its journey to pick up and/or drop off freight cars at industries along the tracks instead of just going straight through. (Photograph by Harold Krewer.)

An eastbound freight train is passing an old grain elevator at El Paso in this 1982 photograph. The elevator was demolished in the 1990s. El Paso is where the TP&W crossed a branch line of the Illinois Central Railroad. The signals for the junction can be seen in the background. (Photograph by Roger A. Holmes.)

An eastbound freight train is crossing Farm Creek, about halfway between Washington and East Peoria, in winter 1982. The train is climbing the infamous Washington Hill, a steep grade out of the Illinois River valley that often posed a great challenge to trains. (Photograph by Roger A. Holmes.)

In this 1983 photograph, two TP&W trains meet at the Farmdale bridge near the East Peoria yard (see page 52). The train at ground level is traveling over the former Nickel Plate Road, now owned by the Norfolk Southern Railway, from East Peoria to Crandall Junction, north of Morton, to access a short TP&W-owned branch line into Morton to serve industries. (Courtesy of the Clark/Finson Collection, Special Collections Center, Bradley University Library.)

An eastbound freight train hits a snowdrift at a crossing near Eureka, Illinois, in December 1983. The winter of 1983–1984 was brutal, with extremely cold temperatures and lots of intense snowstorms. However, that did not stop railroad fans from documenting the final days of TP&W operations. (Photograph by Roger A. Holmes.)

In 1983, it was announced that the TP&W was going to be officially merged into the Santa Fe Railway effective at midnight on January 1, 1984. On December 31, 1983, many photographers came to the area to document the last day of the railroad. This photograph shows a switcher locomotive in East Peoria on the last day of operations. (Photograph by Harold Krewer.)

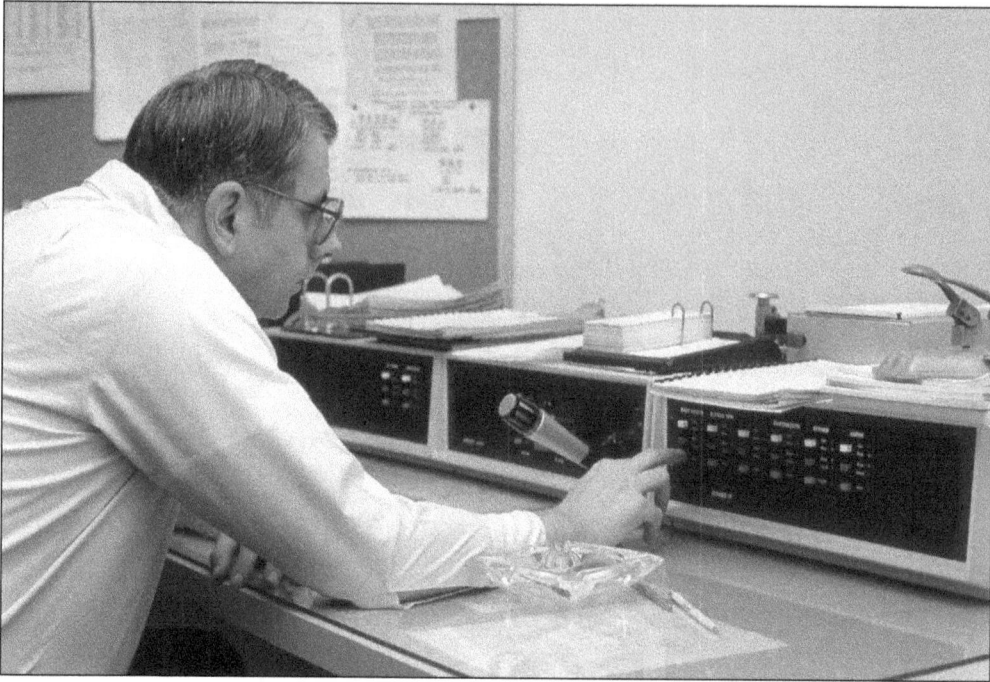

A few minutes before midnight on January 1, 1984, dispatcher John Stell set up the radio that was used to communicate with train crews over the entire railroad. When the clock hit midnight, he called out, "Farewell, Tee Pee Willie, we have lost a friend." (Photograph by Harold Krewer.)

This photograph was taken a few minutes after midnight on January 1, 1984, at the East Peoria yard. The TP&W had positioned several locomotives in various spots for photographers earlier in the night. At the time this picture was taken, the railroad no longer existed and was officially a part of the Santa Fe system. (Photograph by Harold Krewer.)

Six

REVIVAL

In the late 1980s, the Santa Fe decided that the former Toledo, Peoria & Western property was unnecessary for its operations. Talks of selling the property began around 1986. Guy L. Brenkman, president of Pioneer Railcorp, a holding company that owned another local railroad, wanted the TP&W for his system very badly. Other parties expressed great interest in it as well. In the end, it was sold to the Toledo, Peoria & Western Railway Corporation, a new company started by Gordon Fuller and Mike Smith, two businessmen with railroad experience from the northeastern United States. When the new company took over the property, it acquired several former Santa Fe locomotives, as the original TP&W locomotives had either been sold to other railroads or were being retained by the Santa Fe. The president of the "reincarnated" TP&W, Gordon Fuller, had worked for the New York Central Railroad years before, so a handful of the former Santa Fe engines that the new TP&W acquired were painted into a New York Central–inspired paint scheme to honor his former employer. Initially, multiple problems delayed the sale of the railroad, but it was finally able to begin operations in 1989. The new TP&W's operations as an independent company were very short-lived, lasting only until 1996, when a larger company purchased a controlling interest and began to operate it as a subsidiary. In 1999, it was sold outright to RailAmerica, a holding company that owned many railroads around the world.

A Santa Fe freight train hits a snowdrift on the former TP&W near Secor, Illinois, in the winter of 1985, after the Santa Fe had taken over the property. The engineer of this train was Bob Lee, who started his railroading career on the TP&W in 1963, transferred to the Santa Fe after the merger in 1984, and continued to work after the railroad was sold again. Now retired, Lee recently shared a great story about his time on the TP&W. Once, he was working on an eastbound train that had to stop in Piper City, Illinois, to let another train pass. While waiting for the other train, he walked across the street to get a haircut. While he was getting his haircut, an angry railroad manager suddenly burst into the barbershop and yelled at him, demanding to know why he was getting a haircut on company time. Lee responded, "Well, my hair grew on company time, so I'm going to get it cut on company time." (Photograph by Roger A. Holmes.)

TOLEDO, PEORIA & WESTERN RY. CORP.

1990 E. Washington St.
E. Peoria, IL 61611

Telephone 1-800-727-8927

M. A. KATRICKA
   Chief Special Agent

R. M. BUNGARD
   Gen. Foreman, Locomotives & Cars

B. G. SYKES
   Chief Engineer

D. F. MONTGOMERY
   Agent

TRAIN DISPATCHERS

   C. G. Reeser
   T. E. Waldon
   C. H. Waller
   E. E. Wyss
   R. A. Holmes

M. V. SMITH
   Vice President-Hollis, N. H.

C. O'CONNOR
   Vice President-Hollis, N. H.

J. T. MOHN
   Terminal Manager-Hoosierlift, IN

Make Safety A Habit

TOLEDO, PEORIA & WESTERN RAILWAY CORPORATION

TIMETABLE

No. 1

TAKES EFFECT
SUNDAY, MAY 21, 1989
AT 12:01 A.M.
CENTRAL TIME

G. R. FULLER
   President

T. R. MASON
   Vice President-Operations

R. D. PETERSON
   Superintendent

V. L. HAVEL
   Trainmaster

This timetable from May 1989 was the first published following the acquisition of the TP&W by the new Toledo, Peoria & Western Railway Corporation after the Santa Fe decided to sell it. The new company was a non-union entity, and many employees left over from the original TP&W and Santa Fe did not approve of this. They protested the new company taking over and when offered a job at the new company, most of them turned it down. In the end, only a handful of employees stayed with the railroad while the rest found new jobs elsewhere. Due to the lack of manpower, the new company was almost unable to begin operations. (Author's collection.)

Locomotive 2002 is at Hoosierlift near Remington, Indiana, on May 19, 1995. Engineer Randy Brandt is sitting in the cab window. No. 2002 was built in 1961 for the Santa Fe and was sold to the TP&W in 1989. It was sold again in 1999 and eventually wound up in Bay City, Michigan, where it was scrapped. (Photograph by Albert Reinschmidt, author's collection.)

While some of the new TP&W's locomotives were painted in New York Central colors, others remained in the paint scheme of the Santa Fe, their previous owner before coming to the TP&W. This photograph shows some engines in Santa Fe paint at Hoosierlift. (Photograph by Bruce Emmons, courtesy of Jason Jordan.)

In the 1980s, the Santa Fe and Southern Pacific Railroads proposed a merger. Several locomotives on each railroad were painted into a new red and yellow color scheme in preparation for the merger; however, the plan never came to be. This locomotive, painted in the "Kodachrome" scheme, wound up under TP&W ownership in 1989. (Photograph by Roger A. Holmes.)

An eastbound freight train passes through Gridley, Illinois, in October 1989 shortly after the new TP&W company had taken over the property from the Santa Fe. Locomotive No. 2001, pictured here, was severely damaged in a 1990 wreck at Washington, Illinois. (Photograph by Steve Smedley.)

In the 1980s and 1990s, the Chatsworth Historical Society hosted an annual Railroad Days festival in Chatsworth, Illinois, on the anniversary of the 1887 wreck. During the event, the TP&W supplied a locomotive and caboose to give rides out to the wreck site. The 1992 festival featured locomotive No. 2003, pictured here. (Author's collection.)

In 1992, the TP&W purchased this streamlined F7 type diesel locomotive from the Bessemer & Lake Erie Railroad. It was used on freight trains and special inspection and excursion trains over the railroad until 1998, when it was sold. Train crews did not like this locomotive because it was more difficult to climb in and out of than others. (Photograph by Steve Smedley.)

Several years after the original TP&W was merged into the Santa Fe, a former TP&W boxcar that had been sold to a new owner but had not yet been repainted made an appearance at the East Peoria yard. Several freight cars from the original TP&W are still in daily service today. (Photograph by Jerry Reinmann, courtesy of Jason Jordan.)

An eastbound inspection train passes through the hamlet of Marietta, Illinois, near Bushnell in the summer of 1990. The town of Marietta is to the north of this location, but the railroad established a depot here in the mid-1800s to serve the town. (Photograph by Steve Smedley, courtesy of John Stell.)

Many of the locomotives from the original TP&W that had been sold prior to the Santa Fe takeover in 1984 were being used by other companies around the country during the 1980s and 1990s. No. 401, still in TP&W paint, was employed by a Freeport, Illinois, grain elevator as a switch engine at the time of this 1984 photograph. (Author's collection.)

After taking over the TP&W, the Santa Fe retained a handful of the newer TP&W locomotives for use on its system. They were all repainted into Santa Fe colors and received new numbers. Santa Fe No. 2964, formerly TP&W No. 1000, was destroyed in a wreck at Pico Rivera, California, in 1988. (Courtesy of John Stell.)

In December 1986, the Keokuk Junction Railway (KJRY), a small railroad based in Keokuk, Iowa, purchased part of the former TP&W line that ran from Keokuk to La Harpe, Illinois. Beyond La Harpe, the railroad was retained by the TP&W, but not for long. In December 2000, the TP&W decided to get rid of the rest of its western route from the Peoria area westward. Beginning in late 2001, a new operator, the Santa Fe & Lamy Railroad, took over operating duties west of Peoria. In 2005, the line was sold to the KJRY, which still owns and operates it today. While the KJRY now owns the entire former TP&W system west of Peoria, the line east of Peoria is still owned and operated by the TP&W. (Photograph by John Stell.)

For a few years in the 1990s, the KJRY used a handful of antique interurban electric railway cars for special excursion trips over its line between Keokuk and La Harpe. This photograph from 1996 shows two of the cars awaiting their next trip at the Keokuk rail yards. (Photograph by John Stell.)

After acquiring the former TP&W line to La Harpe, the KJRY began using this former TP&W depot as an office building. La Harpe would eventually become the location of the KJRY's main rail yard and shop facilities. (Photograph by John Stell.)

In 1995, the Delaware-Otsego Corporation, a railroad holding company based in New York, purchased a controlling interest in the TP&W. It acquired full control of the railroad in 1996. Delaware-Otsego also owned the New York, Susquehanna & Western (NYSW) Railway, so NYSW-painted locomotives began appearing on the TP&W shortly after Delaware-Otsego gained full control of it. (Author's collection.)

This February 1999 photograph shows an eastbound train near Secor, Illinois, a small community named after Charles A. Secor, an early railroad manager. The leading locomotive is painted in Delaware-Otsego's NYSW color scheme. Within a few months of this photograph, the railroad was acquired by RailAmerica. (Photograph by Steve Smedley.)

In September 1999, the TP&W was sold again to RailAmerica, a holding company that owned several regional railroads around the country. RailAmerica removed much of the corporate identity that was left of both the "reincarnated" TP&W and the original TP&W. Most notably, several of the East Peoria shop buildings dating to the George McNear era were demolished, and most of the locomotives left over from the new TP&W of the 1990s were scrapped. New locomotives arrived on the property to replace them. These new engines were painted in a bland red, white, and blue scheme that was shared by other railroads owned by RailAmerica. While it was still known as the Toledo, Peoria & Western, much of its uniqueness had been lost forever. This photograph shows a RailAmerica train on the TP&W crossing the Farmdale bridge near East Peoria. (Photograph by Jason Jordan.)

An eastbound freight train is parked at the Hoosierlift yard outside of Remington in January 2003. Hoosierlift is still owned by the TP&W today and is currently used as one of the main yards on the railroad. (Photograph by Bruce Emmons, courtesy of Jason Jordan.)

In addition to some of the shop buildings at East Peoria, another historic TP&W building that was demolished during the RailAmerica era was this shed in Sheldon, Illinois, which was once used for storing speeders, small vehicles used for track maintenance and inspections. (Photograph by Bruce Emmons, courtesy of Jason Jordan.)

An eastbound TP&W train passes Bridge Junction on the south side of Peoria on May 1, 2011. Bridge Junction is immediately west of the Peoria & Pekin Union Railway's bridge over the Illinois River, which TP&W trains started to utilize after the 1970 barge accident that destroyed its bridge. (Photograph by Jesse Berryhill.)

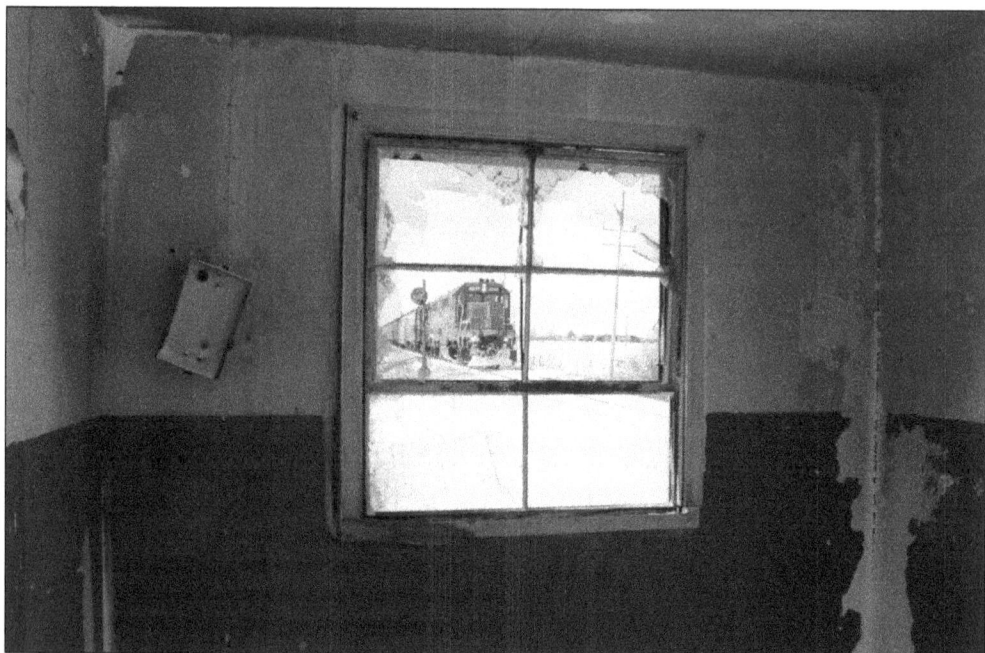

A train approaches an abandoned interlocking tower building at Webster, a small point on the railroad west of Sheldon, Illinois, where the TP&W crosses the Kankakee, Beaverville & Southern Railroad, whose tracks were originally owned by the Chicago, Milwaukee, St. Paul & Pacific Railroad. The interlocking tower once controlled train movements over this junction. (Photograph by Jesse Berryhill.)

In July 2011, the Fort Wayne Railroad Historical Society of New Haven, Indiana, brought its historic Nickel Plate Road steam locomotive No. 765 back to the TP&W. Unlike the locomotive's previous visit in 1980 (see page 81), the 765 was not pulling a public excursion train. This time, it was only using the TP&W east of Peoria as a way to get to a special railroad event in Rock Island, Illinois. Once the train got to Peoria, it turned north onto the Iowa Interstate Railroad for the rest of the trip to Rock Island. The train took the same way back after the event, and this photograph shows the 765 gliding across the Farmdale bridge near East Peoria on its return trip to Indiana. (Photograph by Steve Smedley.)

An eastbound Ringling Brothers circus train is near Secor, Illinois. All locomotives owned by RailAmerica were acquired secondhand from other railroads. While most received RailAmerica's red, white, and blue paint scheme, some units, such as this one from the Southern Pacific Railroad, remained in the paint from their predecessor companies. (Photograph by Steve Smedley.)

A TP&W locomotive is pulling a short train of 13 hopper cars full of corn into Peoria on March 6, 2011. The train was heading to the Archer-Daniels-Midland ethanol plant along the Illinois River. The TP&W still serves the plant today. (Photograph by Steve Smedley.)

Seven

PRESERVATION

Robert McMillan, the original Toledo, Peoria & Western's final president before the company was merged into the Santa Fe in 1984, was a railroad and history fan in his spare time and got interested in the TP&W's history when he became president. Because of his interest, he made a serious effort to preserve as much of the railroad's equipment as possible before the Santa Fe took over. The Santa Fe was interested in using some of the TP&W's newer locomotives, but the cabooses and older locomotives were deemed unnecessary. If these unneeded trains were not off the property by the time the merger took place, they were likely going to be cut up for scrap. Fearing this would happen, McMillan sold and donated as much of the equipment as he could. One locomotive, No. 400, was donated to the Illinois Railway Museum of Union, Illinois, and almost all of the cabooses were sold to railroad fans for preservation. Additional equipment was preserved in the following years, and today, historical TP&W equipment has been preserved all over the state of Illinois. In addition, 1982 saw the formation of the Toledo, Peoria & Western Historical Society, a group that collects and preserves smaller TP&W artifacts such as paperwork and photographs. Thanks to the efforts of Robert McMillan and the TP&W Historical Society, the railroad is well represented in the world of preservation.

As mentioned in chapter three, George McNear owned a fleet of passenger cars to travel over his railroad with fellow executives. After he died in 1947, all but one of those cars were scrapped. The car that was not scrapped was car No. 1, which is now preserved at the Wheels O' Time Museum in Dunlap, Illinois. (Photograph by the author.)

In 1957, ten years after George McNear's death, car No. 1 was sold to Pete Vonachen, owner of a railroad-themed restaurant in Peoria. The car was relocated to the restaurant and remodeled to serve as a dining room. It was donated to the Wheels O' Time Museum in 2011 and is currently being restored to appear as it did when it was used by George McNear. (Photograph by the author.)

In 1983, the TP&Ws depot in Bushnell, Illinois, was moved to the Western Illinois Threshers park near Hamilton, Illinois, for use as a museum. The depot was originally built at Marietta, Illinois, but was moved to Bushnell after the original Bushnell depot burned. Today, the depot has been restored and houses a small museum. (Photograph by the author.)

The depot from Burnside, Illinois, was also relocated to the Western Illinois Threshers park in 1983. Built in 1906, the depot was threatened with demolition, but it was saved and moved to Hamilton. It is currently located a couple hundred feet west of the Bushnell depot and is used for storage. (Photograph by the author.)

The depot in El Paso, Illinois, was at a junction with the Illinois Central Railroad. Also threatened, it was saved in 1994 just hours from its planned demolition and moved back from the tracks. It was restored over the next couple of years and has housed numerous businesses since then. (Photograph by the author.)

Unfortunately, not all TP&W preservation efforts were successful. In 1971, the Piper City Civic Association acquired its local TP&W depot dating to 1876. After briefly using it as a community center, it became apparent that it needed serious repairs to keep it structurally sound. Not enough money to fund the repairs could be raised, so the depot was demolished in September 1979. (Author's collection.)

One of the original TP&W cabooses dating to the 1950s had a second career on the new TP&W of the 1990s. No. 523, built in 1956, was acquired by the Chatsworth Historical Society in Chatsworth, Illinois. Through the efforts of the Chatsworth Historical Society and the TP&W Historical Society, the caboose was restored and saw use on several excursion trips over the TP&W and Bloomer Line, a railroad that crosses the TP&W in Chatsworth, throughout the early 1990s. Once, while being stored at the East Peoria yard, a fire broke out inside the caboose and severely damaged the interior. Both historical societies were able to repair it and continued to operate the caboose for several more years. Today, No. 523 is on static display in downtown Chatsworth and is maintained by the Chatsworth Historical Society. (Photograph by the author.)

While most of the TP&W's depots were demolished in the 1960s and 1970s, towns along the railroad retained small trackside signs with the town name on them. These were known as station signs, even though they had nothing to do with a depot building. Today, many of these station signs are still along the tracks, such as this one in Chatsworth. (Photograph by the author.)

In 1983, Virgil Reeves, a farmer from El Paso, Illinois, purchased caboose 504 for display on his farm. It was removed from the tracks at Enright, a ghost town about halfway between El Paso and Gridley, and trucked to Virgil's farm. When it arrived, he held a "caboose warming" party. Reeves passed away in 2000, but his family continues to maintain the caboose. (Photograph by Connor Taylor.)

Diesel locomotive No. 400 was donated to the Illinois Railway Museum of Union, Illinois, in 1983. For a few years, it pulled excursion trains at the museum before it was taken out of service due to mechanical issues. Today, it is on static display. (Photograph by Brandon Osika.)

The Illinois Railway Museum also owns diesel locomotive No. 800. In 1983, it was sold to the Morristown & Erie Railroad in New Jersey along with locomotive No. 801. The Morristown & Erie retired both locomotives in 2017 and sold the 800 to the museum. The locomotive arrived at the museum in early 2018 and is currently used occasionally to pull excursion trains. (Photograph by Brandon Osika.)

The depot in Forrest, Illinois, was built in 1893 at a junction between the TP&W and the Wabash Railroad. The Wabash line was abandoned in 1991. Recently, the Forrest Historical Society restored the depot and adjacent grounds to become a museum. (Photograph by the author.)

During 2020, when most of the world was shut down due to the COVID-19 pandemic, work to preserve a historic TP&W caboose was underway. Caboose No. 506 was built in October 1940. In July 2020, it was moved from its longtime home on a farm near Fairbury, Illinois, to Toluca, Illinois, where it is being restored to its former glory. (Photograph by the author.)

Eight

THE TP&W TODAY

On December 28, 2012, RailAmerica, then-owner of the Toledo, Peoria & Western, was acquired by Genesee & Wyoming, a holding company that owns regional railroads all over the world. Genesee & Wyoming kept the TP&W name and even used the historic diamond logo on locomotives to pay homage to the previous owners of the company. Under its ownership, many improvements have been made to the TP&W. Track has been upgraded and repaired, and additional trackage has been acquired through a lease to expand operations to Kokomo, Indiana. Freight business is in a good state, with many industries along the TP&W utilizing the railroad for service. In recent years, a wind farm near Chenoa, Illinois, has used the railroad for bringing in wind turbine components, perhaps the most interesting freight the TP&W has ever handled. The Keokuk Junction Railway, which operates the former western end of the TP&W from Peoria to Keokuk, is also doing very well today. With both the TP&W and KJRY in good states financially and physically, operations on both railroads are ensured to continue for many years to come. The TP&W has been well documented by photographers in the 21st century and remains a favorite railroad to photograph. It is likely that the businessmen who formed the Peoria & Oquawka in 1849 would be very pleased to know that their railroad is still operating today and has positively impacted the American railroading scene for over 170 years.

Taken shortly after Genesee & Wyoming took over the TP&W, this photograph shows a westbound train near El Paso, Illinois. This type of railroad photography is called "pacing," where a photographer drives alongside a moving train and captures photographs that show its motion. Route 24 closely parallels the TP&W east of Peoria, allowing for many beautiful pacing shots. (Photograph by Steve Smedley.)

A freight train crosses Farm Creek in East Peoria on March 5, 2019. The train is on the Peoria & Pekin Union Railway, continuing a practice that began in 1970 after the TP&W negotiated trackage rights over the P&PU bridge following the loss of its bridge over the Illinois River. (Photograph by Steve Smedley.)

Last used in the mid-1980s, the historic depot at Effner was a favorite "photo stop" for railroad fans for many years. The abandoned building remained standing into late 2021, when strong winds caused a portion of it to collapse. It was deemed a safety hazard and demolished on December 14. (Photograph by the author.)

While the Effner depot is now gone, a small yard dating to the steam locomotive era is still in place nearby. This photograph from New Year's Eve 2020 shows locomotives 3442 and 3441 parked in the yard waiting for a new assignment after the holiday. (Photograph by the author.)

On November 29, 2020, the TP&W operated a westbound freight train from Gilman to East Peoria. The author and fellow railroad photographer Noah Haggerty were able to photograph the train as it made its way west. It is seen here passing through Piper City, Illinois. (Photograph by the author.)

At Weston, Illinois, the train passed the site of a September 18, 1971, wreck that resulted in 38 freight cars derailing in the downtown area. A fire soon broke out among the wreckage, but thankfully, unlike the Crescent City wreck the previous year, the fire was contained to the derailment area. (Photograph by the author.)

Locomotive 3442 is passing through downtown Chenoa, Illinois. Behind the photographer is a junction with the former Chicago & Alton Railroad, which is now owned by the Union Pacific Railroad. The TP&W has a connection track nearby to the Union Pacific that allows the two railroads to exchange freight cars. (Photograph by Noah Haggerty.)

During the summer of 2020, a new regularly scheduled train, the Fairbury Local, began operations between Fairbury, Illinois, and points east and west. Most TP&W trains do not run on schedules, so this train was well-liked by railroad fans because it was easy to figure out when it was going to operate. Unfortunately, due to a lack of manpower, the run was abolished after just a couple of months. (Photograph by the author.)

When the TP&W was merged into the Santa Fe in 1984, locomotive 402, which had been rebuilt into a special snowplow car, was sold to the Kankakee, Beaverville & Southern (KBS) Railroad, which continues to use the plow today. When not in use, it is stored in Beaverville, Illinois. (Photograph by the author.)

In 1983, the TP&W began utilizing trackage rights over the Norfolk Southern Railway from East Peoria to Morton, Illinois, where the TP&W owns a small branch line to serve industries. This operation is still active today. This TP&W train is at Crandall Junction just north of Morton, where the TP&W branch line meets the Norfolk Southern. (Photograph by Steve Smedley.)

Civer, Illinois, is one of several ghost towns along the TP&W. Just west of Canton, the tracks through Civer are now owned by the Keokuk Junction Railway. At one time, there was an active depot here, but today, only a historical marker and the railroad tracks remain. (Photograph by Connor Taylor.)

From 2005 to 2019, the Keokuk Junction Railway used three historic streamlined diesel locomotives in regular freight service, which earned it national recognition among railroad photographers. This photograph shows the locomotives in Canton, Illinois. In August 2019, they were retired, and in 2020, they were sold. (Photograph by Connor Taylor.)

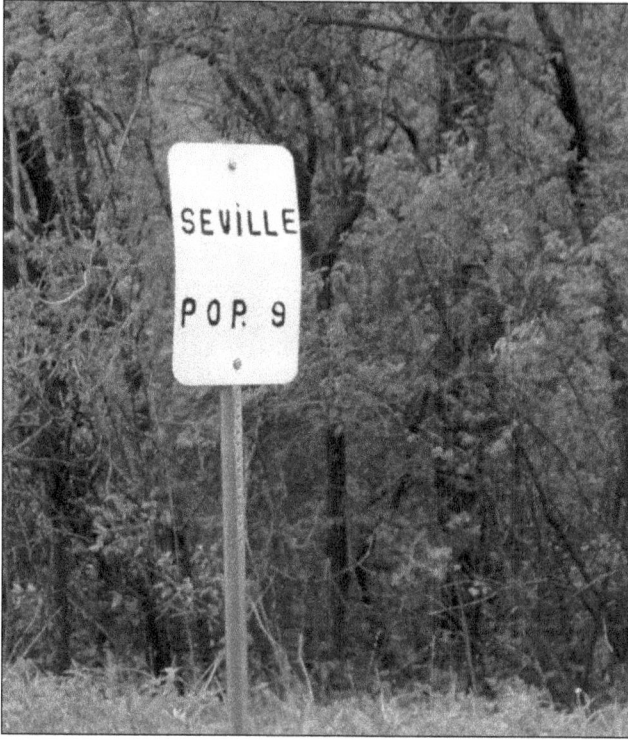

Seville is one of the smallest communities along the portion of the TP&W that is now owned by the Keokuk Junction Railway. This photograph shows the population sign at the entrance to the village, which is along the Spoon River. (Photograph by the author.)

There is still evidence that the railroad through Seville was once owned by the TP&W. This shed was built in the late 1870s. While no longer used, it remains standing, providing a glimpse into Seville's railroad history. At one time, there was also a depot nearby. (Photograph by the author.)

In September 2013, the historic TP&W bridge over the Spoon River at Seville was destroyed in a derailment. Nobody was injured, but the wreck resulted in the bridge being knocked into the river along with several freight cars. Cleanup soon commenced, and a replacement bridge was brought in from Texas. This 2021 photograph shows the replacement. (Photograph by Connor Taylor.)

This timed exposure from the night of September 27, 2021, shows a westbound Keokuk Junction train approaching Glasford, Illinois. The train is bound for Kolbe, just north of Mapleton, Illinois, where the Keokuk Junction operates a small rail yard and shop complex at the entrance to the Kolbe Industrial Spur (see page 68). (Photograph by the author.)

While the TP&W's tracks through La Harpe are now owned by the Keokuk Junction Railway, several remnants of the railroad's previous owner remain, including this small shed built by the TP&W in the late 1800s. (Photograph by the author.)

On January 22, 2021, this historic switch stand was still in use along the Keokuk Junction Railway. The device is used for operating switches, which direct trains down different tracks. It is likely that this switch stand dates to the era when the TP&W still operated this portion of the line. (Photograph by the author.)

This photograph, taken through a ladder on the side of a hopper car, shows a westbound Keokuk Junction train slowly rolling through Elvaston, Illinois. During the steam locomotive era, TP&W trains came through Elvaston at speeds up to 60 miles per hour. (Photograph by the author.)

As of 2021, the original TP&W had been gone for 37 years. Surprisingly, this hopper car from the original railroad still exists. While faded, it is still adorned in its original red TP&W paint from when it was built. (Photograph by the author.)

Looking west down the TP&W tracks into the sunset, this scene has been repeated thousands of times during the more than 170 years of the Toledo, Peoria & Western and its predecessors. Thanks to the hardworking men and women of the railroad, the supportive communities along the tracks, and the prospering railroad industry in the United States, it is very likely that this scene will continue to be repeated for many years to come. (Photograph by the author.)

ABOUT THE TP&W HISTORICAL SOCIETY

In 1982, Glenn Pizer of Morocco, Indiana, established the Toledo, Peoria & Western Historical Society, dedicated to preserving and sharing the history of the TP&W. The group quickly grew, and by 1985, there were members from all over the world. Jerry Reinmann, the police chief of Eureka, Illinois, and a TP&W fan, became president of the society a few years later. Under his direction, the society took off and hosted and participated in numerous TP&W-related events throughout the 1990s. Sadly, in 2004, Jerry Reinmann became ill and passed away. Shortly after, the society went defunct. In 2018, there was a lot of interest in starting a new TP&W Historical Society, so author Thomas Dyrek restarted the organization. Today, the TP&W Historical Society has dozens of members and publishes a biannual newsletter with articles and historic photographs of the Toledo, Peoria & Western and related railroads. For more information about the TP&W Historical Society, email tpwhistorical@gmail.com or follow the society on Facebook.

DISCOVER THOUSANDS OF LOCAL HISTORY BOOKS FEATURING MILLIONS OF VINTAGE IMAGES

Arcadia Publishing, the leading local history publisher in the United States, is committed to making history accessible and meaningful through publishing books that celebrate and preserve the heritage of America's people and places.

Find more books like this at
www.arcadiapublishing.com

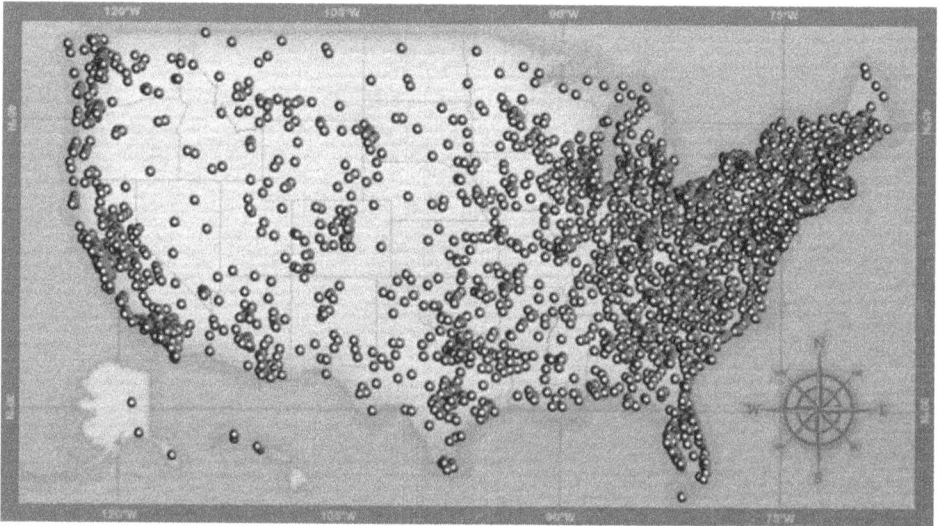

Search for your hometown history, your old stomping grounds, and even your favorite sports team.